THE CEREMONIAL CITY

THE
CEREMONIAL CITY

TOULOUSE OBSERVED

1738–1780

ROBERT A. SCHNEIDER

PRINCETON UNIVERSITY PRESS

PRINCETON, NEW JERSEY

Library of Congress Cataloging-in-Publication Data

Schneider, Robert Alan.
The ceremonial city : Toulouse observed, 1738–1780 /
Robert A. Schneider
p.   cm.
Includes bibliographical references and index.
ISBN 0-691-03465-6
ISBN 0-691-03464-8 (pbk.)
1. Toulouse (France)—History.   2. Rites and ceremonies—France—Toulouse—
History—18th century.   3. Barthès, Pierre, b. 1704. Heures perdues.   I. Title.
DC801.T726S35 1994
944´.862—dc20   94-26081

This book has been composed in Adobe Garamond
Designed by Jan Lilly

Princeton University Press books are printed on acid-free paper
and meet the guidelines for permanence and durability of the
Committee on Production Guidelines for Book Longevity
of the Council on Library Resources

Second printing, and first paperback printing, 1996

Printed in the United States of America
by Princeton Academic Press

2 4 6 8 10 9 7 5 3

For Sarah and Kate

CONTENTS

ACKNOWLEDGMENTS

EVEN SHORT books do not write themselves, and this one, though largely a labor of love, still needed help at every stage. I completed a first draft during a stay in Paris in 1989–1990, supported by grants from the National Endowment for the Humanities and the American Council of Learned Societies. In one form or another, much of the material was presented to several audiences, whose forbearance and comments were most appreciated: the departments of history at Brandeis University and the University of California at Davis; the seminar titled "Popular Culture in Early Modern Europe" at the Folger Library in Washington, D.C.; Robert Descimon's seminar at the Ecole des Hautes Etudes en Sciences Sociales in Paris; and the Society of French Historians conference in Los Angeles, California. In particular, I have profited immensely from the comments and criticisms of David Bien, Tom Brennan, Lawrence Bryant, James Collins, Robert Forster, Mack Holt, and Charles Tilly. Once again, Phil Benedict has proven a critic—and friend—par excellence. I fear that I have not managed to incorporate all his criticisms and suggestions into the final version of the book, but I hope that he, and others who so generously shared their thoughts with me, will not find their efforts wasted. In any case, they have my thanks. All the book's errors and excesses are entirely of my own making.

Christian Peligry supplied me with a microfilm of the Barthès diary, and the staff of the Bibliothèque municipale de Toulouse have been ever-helpful. (I thus forgive them for making me wear a pair of tight-fitting white gloves when I first consulted "Les heures perdues de Pierre Barthès" in the un-air-conditioned Toulouse library one sweltering summer several years ago.) Jack Thomas of the University of Toulouse-Mirail continues to be my eyes and legs in Toulouse, as he has been for over ten years now. Michel Taillefer, also of Toulouse-Mirail, kindly furnished me with some interesting information about Barthès.

At Princeton University Press I have been fortunate in the support and cooperation of Lauren Osborne and Lauren Lepow.

Sarah Mitchell helped in the proofreading, and has served as a sounding board for my thoughts about Barthès's diary for most of our, admittedly short, married life. That that life continues to be rich and eventful has nothing to do with him and everything to do with her and our treasure, Kate.

THE CEREMONIAL CITY

INTRODUCTION

AMONG THE documents in the manuscript collection of the Municipal Library of Toulouse are eight notebooks of varying size, all bound in the eighteenth century. They comprise the diary of Pierre Barthès, an obscure tutor of Latin who kept a record of what he believed to be the notable events that occurred in his city of Toulouse between 1738 and 1780. For all Barthès's obscurity (and he was obscure; without his diary we would know almost nothing about him), his notebooks have hardly been gathering dust these past two centuries. Virtually every historian of eighteenth-century Toulouse has consulted them—Robert Forster for his study of the local nobility, David D. Bien for his book *The Calas Affair*, Michel Taillefer for his *thèse* on the Freemason lodges of Toulouse, and others.[1] I too found Barthès's "Les heures perdues"[2] an indispensable source for the last part of my book *Public Life in Toulouse 1463–1789*.[3] Although I certainly did not believe that I had exhausted Toulouse's rich history and archives in writing that lengthy monograph, I had resolved, with some misgivings, to leave it to others to mine its historical treasures. But then

---

[1] Robert Forster, *The Nobility of Toulouse in the Eighteenth Century* (Baltimore, 1960); David D. Bien, *The Calas Affair: Persecution, Toleration and Heresy in Eighteenth-Century Toulouse* (Princeton, 1960); Michel Taillefer, *La franc-maçonnerie toulousaine: 1741–99* (Paris, 1984).
[2] Bibliothèque municipale de Toulouse, MS 699–706. Henceforth, these manuscripts will be cited by volume and page numbers only. A highly abridged and unreliable version of Barthès's diary was published early in this century: E. Lamouzèle, *Toulouse au XVIIIe siècle d'après les "Heures Perdues" de Pierre Barthès* (Toulouse, 1914).
[3] Ithaca, 1989.

Barthès's diary made me think otherwise. For while he had been exploited as a witness of various aspects of social life in his city, no one had ever approached his diary as a source for the wide range of ceremonies, rituals, and festivities that fill the bulk of its pages.[4] This short book is an attempt to do just that.

Indeed, this view of the "ceremonial city" is, as the book's subtitle indicates, based on one man's view. I am aware that such an approach runs the risk of blinkering my field of vision insofar as it largely, although not entirely, ignores other sources. But the fact is that evidence on ceremonial life is somewhat scarce in most institutional records. Municipal and ecclesiastical archives abound in serial evidence on such matters as elections, judicial proceedings and crimes, taxes and finance, parish visits, property holdings, poor relief, baptisms, marriages and deaths, and the like. But it was rare for an institution to leave behind comprehensive records of its ceremonial history, and rarer still to find such a record for a whole city. Hence the uniqueness of Barthès's diary.

Why concentrate on ceremonial life? A once prevalent prejudice had it that collective expressive activities, especially celebrations and rituals, are less than crucial for social analysis— that what people do elsewhere, in politics, at work, or in family life, is far more important and fundamental than what they do on festive or celebratory occasions. Most historians would now reject this view. A common feature of a whole range of recent trends in social history—from the study of popular culture and *mentalité* to the New Cultural History and the so-called linguistic turn—is a concern with symbolic forms and expressive life, including public rituals and ceremonies. For it is now appreciated that these are formative ele-

---

[4] The exception being Michel Cassan, "La fête à Toulouse au dix-huitième siècle" (Thèse 3ème cycle, Université de Toulouse-Mirail, 1980).

ments of people's worldviews, particular interests, and collective identities, and not merely reflections of material or social realities.

Most historical attention, however, has focused on the ritual aspect of popular culture and those carnivalesque rites that celebrated a "world turned upside down." As important as these rites were in articulating the desires and values of ordinary people, indeed in constituting the culture that lent meaning to their lives and defended their communities as well, they were only a portion of the ceremonial repertory that constituted public life in the Old Regime. For the most part, Barthès's diary celebrates another order of ceremony—the public rituals and festivities that regularly punctuated Toulouse's official ceremonial calendar. While he does note some of the more bizarre displays that made up Toulouse's lively street culture, his primary interest is in those sanctioned political and religious ceremonies that expressed the values and projected the authority of the Old Regime establishment.

Thus one advantage of Barthès's observations lies in affording us an appreciation not only of the extraordinary weight of ceremony in an Old Regime city—which was impressive if somewhat perplexing to a modern sensibility—but also of its hegemonic role in repeatedly thrusting representations of church and monarchy before the populace. Historians of religion have long been aware of the importance of public devotions, such as processions, to the Catholicism of the masses; and, thanks to Barthès, a true religious enthusiast, we shall have ample opportunity to witness the rich processional regime that flourished in his eighteenth-century city. But we are much less aware of the dimensions of political, as opposed to religious, ceremony as it intruded into the lives of ordinary people. Even with the current interest in the political culture of prerevolutionary France, there has been a notable neglect of its ceremonial aspect.[5] When eighteenth-century historians of political culture have noted the ceremonial face of monarchical rule, they have either assumed its profile diminished or concluded that a decline in the monarchy's prestige and sacredness was evident in its ritual representations.[6]

This is not to say that attention to the ritual and ceremonial aspects of political culture is generally lacking among contemporary historians. On the contrary, in part as a result of a growing appreciation of the symbolic basis of authority, in part as a result of the insight that political constitutions are ceremonial as well as textual in nature—in part too because of the incalculable influence of Clifford Geertz[7]—historians have never before exhibited such an interest in the ritual aspect of politics. This interest has been especially intense for Renaissance Italy and Old Regime France, and the present study would have been inconceivable without works by such historians as Richard Trexler, Edward Muir, Ralph Giesey, Sarah Hanley, and Lawrence Bryant, to name only a few.[8] But

[5] Keith Michael Baker, ed., *The French Revolution and the Creation of Modern Political Culture*, vol. 1, *The Political Culture of the Old Regime* (Oxford, 1987). The exception in this volume is Ralph Giesey, "The King Imagined," pp. 41–59. In her review of the Baker volume, "Politics, Culture, and the Origins of the French Revolution," *Journal of Modern History* 61 (December 1989), Sarah Maza has commented on the scant attention the authors pay "to the tangible, visual, iconic dimensions of political culture, not all of which by any means were confined to Versailles" (p. 721).

[6] The literature is conveniently summarized, and this argument forcefully presented, in Roger Chartier, *The Cultural Origins of the French Revolution*, trans. Lydia G. Cochrane (Durham and London, 1991), chap. 6.

[7] See especially *The Interpretation of Cultures* (New York, 1973) and *Negara: The Theatre State in Nineteenth-Century Bali* (Princeton, 1980).

[8] Richard Trexler, *Public Life in Renaissance Florence* (New York, 1979); Edward Muir, *Civic Ritual in Renaissance Venice* (Princeton, 1981); Ralph E. Giesey, *The Royal Funeral Ceremony in Renaissance France* (Geneva, 1960) and *Cérémonial et puissance souveraine: France, XVIe–XVIIe siècles* (Paris, 1987); Sarah Hanley, *The "Lit de Justice" of the Kings of France* (Princeton, 1983); Lawrence M. Bryant, *The King and the City in the Parisian Royal Entry Ceremony* (Geneva, 1986). Among the many other relevant studies one

though sophisticated and exceedingly erudite, the French studies have, for the most part, given us a partial view of political ceremony—limited to the venues of Versailles and Paris, framed in chronological terms that largely neglect the eighteenth century, and detached from the context of popular perceptions and experiences. Their view thus risks overlooking the vitality of provincial ceremonial displays of the monarchy in the period after Louis XIV. Moreover, their approach implicitly assumes that as the perceived sacredness of the monarchy waned, so too did its majesty and popular appeal. But this is to reason—wrongly, it seems to me—that monarchy could only be effective if framed in religious terms, and, by extension, that monarchical government was fundamentally ill-suited to a developing society. Is this not to read the breakdown of the monarchy and the Revolution backward onto the eighteenth century and thus to diagnose, *post hoc ergo propter hoc*, the political culture of the monarchy strictly in terms of its ill-fated future?

There is, in short, no reason to believe that the ceremonial

---

might cite are Jean-Marie Apostolidès, *Le roi-machine: spectacle et politique au temps de Louis XIV* (Paris, 1981); Colette Beaune, *The Birth of an Ideology: Myth and Symbols of Nation in Late Medieval France* (Berkeley and Los Angeles, 1991); Peter Burke, "Sacred Rulers, Royal Priests: Rituals of the Early Modern Popes," in *The Historical Anthropology of Early Modern Italy: Essays on Perception and Communication* (Cambridge, 1987), pp. 168–82; idem, *The Fabrication of Louis XIV* (New Haven and London, 1992); David Cannadine and Simon Price, eds., *Rituals of Royalty: Power and Ceremonial in Traditional Societies* (Cambridge, 1987); Michèle Fogel, *Les cérémonies de l'information dans la France du XVIe au XVIIIe siècle* (Paris, 1989); Victor E. Graham and W. McAllister Johnson, *The Royal Tour of France by Charles IX and Catherine de Médicis: Festivals and Entries, 1564–1566* (Toronto, 1979); Richard Jackson, *Vive le Roi! A History of the French Coronation from Charles V to Charles X* (Chapel Hill, 1984); Mona Ozouf, *Festivals and the French Revolution*, trans. Alan Sheridan (Cambridge, Mass., 1988); Roy Strong, *Splendor at Court: Renaissance Spectacle and the Theatre of Power* (Boston, 1973); Sean Wilentz, ed., *Rites of Power: Symbolism, Ritual, and Politics since the Middle Ages* (Philadelphia, 1985).

resources of the eighteenth-century monarchy were inadequate to the tasks of promoting its interests and appealing to the populace. And it is simply incorrect, as the best recent historian of revolutionary festivals assumes, that "royal festivities . . . with exemplary rigidity, articulated the hierarchy of rank between corporate persons and bodies"—at least from the perspective of Toulouse.[9] For as we shall see, Barthès's diary demonstrates the robustness, even novelty, of royal festivities, where fluidity and openness, not "rigidity" and "hierarchy," set the tone. Whether these festivities were effective in buttressing the monarch's prestige in an era when so much was working to undermine it is, of course, another question. And whether these festivities truly managed to engage the people and galvanize their energies is something, in fact, that I shall cast some doubt upon.

The mobilizing potential of ceremony will be one of our main concerns, for I start with the now commonplace assumption, derived from a Durkheimian perspective, that social solidarity has something to do with ritual and festive activities. To be sure, no one would claim that societies or communities are constituted primarily through ritual, but neither should one dismissively assert that symbolic behavior merely reflects the supposedly more fundamental material integuments that hold social groupings together. The assumption, rather, is based upon the realization that social solidarity is an epistemological as well as a social phenomenon—that people have to know and acknowledge their connectedness to others and recognize their collective plight; and that this entails shared experiences which make such a realization possible. Festivities, ceremonies, and rituals are just one means by which this realization can be conveyed and affirmed, but their frequency in early modern society suggests that they played an

[9] Ozouf, *Festivals and the French Revolution*, p. 3.

integral part in establishing (and reestablishing) people's perception of their collective identity. Thus, one of my concerns will be to determine, not only how successful different rituals and ceremonies were in enlisting popular participation, but, perhaps more important, how well they managed to yoke the populace's loyalties to the values they represented.

Because Barthes largely restricted his gaze to the official facet of public life, the approach here will necessarily differ from many current treatments of ceremony and ritual that focus on a rather different realm, that of popular culture. Historians have discovered that a stock feature of early modern popular ritual was the dynamic of "inversion"—the topsy-turvy reordering of the social world in ways that mocked the hierarchical status quo, vented the people's normally repressed desires, and celebrated, if only momentarily, an idealized, alternative vision of reality.[10] In examining such inversion rituals as carnival and charivari, historians have borrowed from anthropology, and most prominently the approach of Victor Turner.[11] Turner, himself reworking the theories of Van Gennep, sees many rituals in terms of an antinomy he calls structure and anti-structure (or *communitas*). All societies, he argues, need to experience moments when the hierarchy, the "structure," is momentarily dissolved or suspended, thus allowing participants afterward to reenter the social order bearing with them a renewed sense of community. It is through the movement from structure to *communitas* and back again to structure that societies are able to function and maintain their equilibrium. In his studies, Turner focuses mostly on

[10] Peter Burke, *Popular Culture in Early Modern Europe* (New York, 1978), chap. 7; Natalie Zemon Davis, *Society and Culture in Early Modern France* (Stanford, 1974), chaps. 4 and 6; Mikhail Bakhtin, *Rabelais and His World*, trans. H. T. Iswolsky (Cambridge, Mass., 1968), esp. chap. 3.

[11] For Turner's theories and their applications, see *The Ritual Process: Structure and Anti-Structure* (Chicago, 1969); *Dramas, Fields, and Metaphors* (Ithaca, 1974); and *From Ritual to Theater* (New York, 1982).

rites of passage, but he also sees *communitas* emerging in religious pilgrimages and processions, as well as in the festivities of carnival. All of these rites create experiences that stand in dialectical relationship to society—contrasting diametrically with the given social structure and its constraints while helping to sustain society through their ultimately integrative and restorative powers.

But not all ritual forms lend themselves to the experience of *communitas*; indeed, most appear to reproduce the world "rightside up" and thus would seem to embody the "structure" that is the antithesis of *communitas*. This is certainly the case with those rites and ceremonies that Barthès, a man who identified with his city's hierarchy and official institutions, deemed worthy of recording. How then to think of them? One all too common approach I would like to avoid is to see official ceremony (and throughout I will use the term "ceremony" as a generic catchall for ritual, festivities, and other public displays) as simply a reflection of the social structure, however that might be understood. For this seems to me to be just as limiting, and denigrating of the value of culture, as the crude Marxist distinction between base and superstructure. The task is rather to appreciate the independent force of ceremony as a potentially constitutive factor in the makeup of social reality. To borrow Clifford Geertz's terms, ceremony can function in a dual sense: as a "model of" society—its reflection in symbolic terms; but also as a "model for"—a map or guide for the epistemological process of understanding how society might be patterned.[12] And the assumption in the latter sense is that any society maintains in circulation a variety of patterns that serve as so many lenses through which elements of reality can be configured. Understood in these terms, cere-

---

[12] Geertz, "Religion as a Cultural System," in *The Interpretation of Cultures*, pp. 87–125. See also the insightful remarks of Sherry B. Ortner, *Sherpas through Their Rituals* (Cambridge, 1978), p. 8.

mony functions like language insofar as, in the words of a structural anthropologist, "it molds into articulate thought aspects of reality, breaking-up the continuum of visual experience into sets of categories with distinguishable names and thereby provid[ing] us with a conceptual apparatus for intellectual operations at an abstract and metaphysical level."[13]

Indeed, to liken ceremony to language is one strategy employed by anthropologists to comprehend the nonreductive functioning and meaning of ceremony.[14] For, understood in its structural and poststructural sense, language is not merely a tool wielded in the interest of purposeful expression; rather, it has the capacity to shape our view of the world—to construct reality and to endow it with meanings in ways that often escape our designs. Likewise, ceremonial forms can be seen as idioms for collective behavior that quite differently articulate the terrain of public life, with implications for the construction of social reality. Many ceremonies, especially religious rituals and other official rites, create tightly structured experiences conveying a similarly structured view of social reality. Others, usually those more festive and celebratory in nature, project a more open, less constrained view of the social order. And all ceremonial activity, again like language, remains to some extent indeterminate in its expressiveness, allowing for a variety of often unpredictable responses, interpretations, or "readings."

While ceremony does have a linguistic aspect, many anthropologists have observed that there is a dramatic element

[13] Edmund Leach, "Ritual," in *The International Encyclopedia of the Social Sciences* (New York, 1968), 13:524. See also Claude Lévi-Strauss, *The Savage Mind* (Chicago, 1966); and Pierre Bourdieu, *Outline of a Theory of Practice* (Cambridge, 1977), p. 120.

[14] Maurice Bloch, *Ritual, History and Power: Selected Essays in Anthropology* (Atlantic Highlands, N.J., 1989); Lévi-Strauss, *The Savage Mind*; Mary Douglas, *Purity and Danger: An Analysis of the Concepts of Pollution and Taboo* (London, 1966).

as well.[15] This should not be surprising since the early history of theater was intertwined with ritual life. Like a theatrical performance, most ceremony is temporally and spatially bounded, adheres to a scripted or well-rehearsed procedure, and projects its message—in gestures, words, song, or a combination of all three—in a stylized, often compressed manner. The performative aspect of ceremony recalls J. L. Austin's notion of "performative utterance," most compellingly illustrated in the statement "I do" in the wedding ceremony where the phrase *enacts* a sentiment rather than merely expressing it.[16] One might claim that if anything distinguishes "ritual" from other sorts of ceremonies—especially celebrations and festivities—the difference lies in its strict adherence to this performative dimension. For like theatrical performances, rituals are usually governed by an implicitly scripted, often obsessively attended to, sense of correct enactment. And this implies that any deviation or failure to perform according to script represents a more general failure of the ritual ordering of society itself.

The relevance of thinking about ceremony in terms analogous to language and drama will become apparent when we discuss the two dominant ceremonial forms in the late-eighteenth-century city: public devotions and political, usually monarchical, festivities. In fact, one striking conclusion evident from Barthès's diary is not only how large a shadow these ceremonies cast over Toulouse's public life, but also how very different they were from each other. Most studies of the political culture of the Old Regime emphasize the symbiotic

[15] See the works of Victor Turner, cited above, n. 11; also S. J. Tambiah, "A Performative Approach to Ritual," in his *Culture, Thought, and Social Action* (Cambridge, Mass., 1985), pp. 123–66; and Robert Wuthnow, *Meaning and Moral Order: Explorations in Cultural Analysis* (Berkeley, 1987), pp. 11–15, 343.

[16] J. L. Austin, *How to Do Things with Words* (Cambridge, Mass., 1962).

relationship between Church and State, demonstrating, for example, how the Counter-Reformation church and the absolute monarchy worked as twin centralizing agencies in transforming local and popular culture. And for the prerevolutionary era, the political role of Jansenism, its contribution to the emergence of a constitutionally oriented opposition movement to the crown, has been convincingly argued.[17] I have no intention of contradicting this general view; indeed, much of the evidence contained in Barthès's diary confirms it (especially with regard to the place of the Te Deum in monarchical festivities). But one of the virtues of observing political culture from a local perspective consists in seeing the limitations of and exceptions to generally held assumptions. Though the church was politically and socially implicated in the ruling order of the Old Regime, religious faith remained, as Tocqueville argued, mostly a separate matter.[18] And this is mirrored in the ritual facet of local devotional life. In short, the view from late-eighteenth-century Toulouse casts the ceremonial representations of religion and state in two very separate realms, suggesting that for ordinary people they remained rather distinct categories of experience.

Perhaps the most impressive aspect of the eighteenth-century "ceremonial city" is the sheer magnitude and frequency of public display, whether of a religious, political, or festive nature. The Old Regime is rightly understood as a political and social order highly suspicious of popular mobilization and downright contemptuous of "the people," their culture and interests. Of course, the people noisily and often violently made known their grievances and demands nevertheless. But

[17] Dale Van Kley, "The Jansenist Constitutional Legacy in the French Prerevolution," in Baker, *The Political Culture of the Old Regime*, pp. 169–202.

[18] Alexis de Tocqueville, *The Old Regime and the French Revolution*, trans. Stuart Gilbert (Garden City, N.Y., 1955), pp. 5–9.

they also had a role as participants and spectators in the officially sanctioned displays that periodically marked public life. Religious devotions required active devotees, political festivities required a festive populace, and public executions required the watchful presence of the crowd to legitimate the ultimate judicial act. We are so accustomed to thinking of democracy as the midwife of sanctioned popular participation that we are apt to overlook the routine presence of the people on the ceremonial stage of the Old Regime itself.

These are some of the themes that will guide us as we reconstruct the "ceremonial city" from Barthès's diary. But only a portion of what follows is devoted to issues relating to the public displays that held his attention. The first chapter introduces Barthès, the diarist, and his diary. The second draws upon his text to present a portrait of late-eighteenth-century Toulouse. Chapter 3 turns to the acts of criminal justice, for the most part executions, that drew Barthès's rather macabre interest. The next two chapters are reconstructions of two different clusters of ceremonies that predominate in the pages of his diary: public devotions, especially religious processions both large and small, and a variety of secular and political festivities that increasingly dominated public life in the eighteenth century. In the concluding chapter I pay particular attention to a comparison between religious processions and political festivities as competing ceremonial idioms. There I assess their relative importance and influence in the last decades of the Old Regime, and I suggest a way of understanding the role of ceremony in public life.

Much of what follows is thus a description and reconstruction of festive and ritual life in eighteenth-century Toulouse. It is my hope that the material presented here will be of service to historians and others interested in the subject, to use and reflect upon as they see fit. I hope too that my presentation of this material, in much of its detail and variety, will prove evocative for readers, especially of some of the color and contrast of eighteenth-century city life—for example, the misery that abounded amid growing wealth, the alternating scenes of ritual torment on the scaffold and festive celebration in the streets, the reliance on force majeure in a city where the values of civility were on the rise, or the massive displays of baroque piety that still aroused the spiritual passions of ordinary people in the Age of the Enlightenment. For I remain convinced that analytical history does not have to dispense with a sympathetic rendering of the past. Indeed, it seems to me that even the most sophisticated reader has something to learn simply by confronting the past, and that a fundamental task of any historian is to make this confrontation possible. If the following chapters fulfill that task, I must credit an exasperating, small-minded diarist named Pierre Barthès.

THE OBSERVER AND
HIS DIARY

Ill-fated Day

The thirteenth of this month at ten in the morning my wife, Jeanne Averlence, died after five days of illness. She was buried the next day, the fourteenth of the same, in the cemetery of the Dalbade. She was thirty-three years, five months old, having been born the thirteenth of September, 1707. We had been together eleven years, three months, five days, having been married on January 8, 1730.

"Les heures perdues," April 1741 (699:171)

For the right kind of epilogue to the year 1765, we only need to cast a glance at the diverse epochs that went into it in order to judge the horrors of which it was composed: a dreadful misery is at the base of it, something our descendants will have trouble believing; an intolerable luxury spread indiscriminately among all stations is supported and propped up on this base. A frightful contrast borne out among modest and great alike. A number of do-nothings established throughout the city are responsible for nightly brigandage in houses and shops, without the vigilance of the magistrates having any effect in purging the city of this vermin and assuring the inhabitants some tranquillity in their own homes. The harvest of wheat has dis-

appointed all our hopes, for at the hour I write it is priced between fifteen livres and fifteen livres, ten sous a setier and is going up steadily. . . . Commerce, which is suffering up to the point of being swallowed up, does not give us much more hope for the following years [but] without the monopolists who are everywhere the people would not have suffered a lack of vital necessities. What to do? We must submit to the divine will that, without doubt, wishes this fate for us.

"Les heures perdues," January 1766 (704:6–7)

WE LEARN very little about Pierre Barthès from his diary. He was born on November 2, 1704, to Guillaume Barthès, a fuller, and Anne Marcouly, the daughter of an artisan. His paternal uncle, also a fuller, and a relative of his mother stood as his godparents, bringing him to the baptismal font in Toulouse's church of the Daurade. Only his father and uncle were able to sign their names to the certificate of baptism in the parish register.[1]

As for his childhood and education, we can infer only that he was educated by the Jesuits—hence his fervent loyalty to the teaching fathers and their Society when they were expelled from the city, as from the realm, in 1764. Indeed, he owed his livelihood to the Jesuits, for his education at their college enabled him to advance beyond his father's humble status and take up the position of master tutor of Latin. Barthès was exceedingly proud of his proficiency in Latin and proves something of a show-off—he does not wear his erudition lightly. His diary is sprinkled with Latin phrases and citations from classical authors, which usually serve to mark a disapproving entry or sardonically cap an observation. But his linguistic expertise also had a public utility, for he frequently was engaged by the city to devise the Latin inscriptions that adorned civic festivals and monuments.

In 1730, at twenty-six, Barthès married Jeanne Averlence, twenty-three, who bore him five children, four boys and a girl. Two died in infancy, while another, Jean-Pierre Barthès, left home at seventeen to join the army, just several months before the end of his apprenticeship. In an uncharacteristically personal entry, Barthès condemned his son's precipitous leave-taking as "an act of folly."[2] But his chagrin was soon to be

Unless otherwise indicated, all translations are my own.

[1] 699:8. Barthès discusses these and other autobiographical details at the beginning of his diary.
[2] 699:312.

compounded with grief, for four years later this errant son died of illness in Calais.[3] Barthès notes with obvious pride and tenderness the important events in his children's, as well as his godchildren's, lives, especially their confirmations and marriages, but he does not dwell on family matters. In 1741, only ten years after their marriage, death claimed Barthès's wife, her passing warranting barely a mention in the pages of his diary.[4] In 1754 he married Jean-Marie Gairal, a merchant's widow.[5] At her death nine years later, Barthès recorded the inscription he composed for her tombstone, a testimony to his great grief, which he meditated upon at length, but also further demonstration of his expertise as a Latinist.[6] Barthès seems to have survived most of his relatives, for he dutifully, if sometimes laconically, notes the passing of his parents, aunts, uncles, children, and cousins. He was seventy-six years old when "Les heures perdues" abruptly ends in December 1780, and it is likely that he died shortly thereafter. No entry of decease has been discovered in the city's parish registers.

It was in December 1737, when he was thirty-three, that Barthès began his daily record of public life in Toulouse in the first of what would be the eight notebooks constituting "Les heures perdues." One is tempted to speculate that he undertook the enterprise with a more personal account in mind, for in the first pages he describes a dream he had on the night of March 5, 1738, a revelation all the more striking in the context of a diary so devoid of personal details.[7] In the dream he is attacked by a pack of wild dogs suddenly emerging from the ocean. His wife, upon hearing the dream (he awoke her to recount it to her), begged him not to undertake a planned excursion to the countryside the next day, a suggestion Barthès dismisses with a typically condescending remark about

---

[3] 701:53.   [4] 699:71.   [5] 702:16.
[6] 703:144.   [7] 699:6–7.

her "superstition." In fact, while out walking he was set upon by a dog, an incident which caused him to reflect that "at least in that part the dream was true." Shortly after this entry, Barthès mentions his wife and five children. The dream and this capsule family portrait serve as his entire curriculum vitae.

But if Barthès is reticent about his personal life, his opinions, prejudices, and loyalties about more public matters are apparent on virtually every page. He was not a detached observer, the typical flaneur casting a jaundiced eye on all about him. On the contrary, though a man of middling station and little power, Barthès was passionately concerned about the fate of his city, its inhabitants, and his country. Just as apparent was his identification with the Old Regime establishment. Although his diary relentlessly documents the miseries of the era, never does he display less than total deference to the monarchy and its policies, even as he notes the debilitating effects of new taxes on the populace. The magistrates of the Parlement of Toulouse, the royal court for much of southwestern France and the most powerful corporation in the region, received his unswerving adulation. When the parlement was disbanded by the minister Maupeou in 1771, Barthès bemoaned the year as "the hardest and most horrible ever witnessed in Toulouse since its founding."[8] And when it was reinstated in 1774, his jubilation was unrestrained, matched only by the popular celebrations, which he described at length, that greeted the returning magistrates. Only the Jesuits rivaled the royal magistrates for his affections, and for this reason his loyalties were ultimately pulled in contradictory directions. For it was the parlement that orchestrated the campaign against the Jesuits culminating in their expulsion in 1764. Barthès expressed deep sadness at the loss of his former teachers but, predictably, never ventures a criticism of the par-

[8] 704:170.

lement. One can only surmise that such corporate rivalry between two traditional buttresses of the established order bore
a cost in undermining the social faith of someone as normally
deferential and as identified with the ruling hierarchy as Pierre
Barthès.

His religious faith, however, remained strong. Barthès was
a member of the Company of Gray Penitents and also served
as an officer in a lay confraternity that distributed bread to the
poor of his parish.[9] Unlike a growing number of educated
Frenchmen in the eighteenth century, Barthès manifested an
affiliation with the church more profound than that of a
merely dutiful communicant. As in other matters, he was passionate in his faith, and though he often criticized the superstition and credulity of the common people, he was no cynic.
When supplicatory processions were staged during drought,
flooding, or other natural calamities, for example, he shared
wholeheartedly in the popular belief that relief would result
only from divine intervention. He believed in miracles and
reports the occurrence of several in Toulouse with unblinking
credulity. He detested Protestants with a vengeance and did
not disguise his glee when a Calvinist minister found his way
to the scaffold. David Bien, in his study of the Calas affair,
declares that Barthès was "a bigot, and any age would no
doubt have regarded him as such."[10] And his bigotry was indeed nowhere more apparent than during the trial of Jean
Calas, the Toulouse Calvinist tortured and executed for the
alleged murder of his son. He denounced Calas's supporters
for their "blindness and fanaticism" and expressed outrage
at the news that the English were soliciting donations for
the executed Calvinist's family.[11] But this only confirmed
Barthès's view that "Religion" was everywhere under siege,

[9] 699:211.   [10] Bien, *The Calas Affair*, p. 19.
[11] 703:184.

not only or even primarily by Calvinists, but by the forces of atheism and "libertinage of thought." "Religion mocked, scorned, and dishonored" is one of his favorite refrains. To blame were those "innovators" who led people astray, away from the "faith of our fathers." He was, in short, an implacable opponent of the Enlightenment, and his ceaseless railings against the partisans of free thought and irreligion give evidence that the philosophes' campaign had, by the mid-eighteenth century, penetrated deep into the provincial ranks of the educated. Still, Barthès was somewhat confused about the enemy's identity, for in 1769 he entered an encomium to Voltaire without mention of the philosophe's views on religion or his efforts on behalf of Calas.[12]

But Barthès's complaint was not limited to the apparent waning of faith; his condemnation of society was wholesale, ranging from the hedonism of the rich to the sloth and lawlessness of the lower classes. Barthès was convinced that he lived in the worst of times. To be sure, there was much to bemoan in the latter half of the eighteenth century, especially in a large metropolis such as Toulouse, where crime was on the increase, the price of bread escalated steadily, and food riots frequently disturbed the public peace. Barthès was particularly alert to the rise in price of victuals, carefully monitoring the inflation in his résumé of each year; and he reveals himself as something of a materialist, for his annual evaluation was largely colored by the level of prices, the single most important determinant of the populace's fortunes. If a materialist, he was also an anticapitalist, decrying those grain merchants—"public bloodsuckers," he repeatedly called them—whose perfectly legal commercial dealings he blamed for the recurrent dearth in the city's markets. But his criticisms were general, hardly limited to the economic difficulties of the day,

[12] 704:118.

23

and his diary is one long example of what has been called the "enduring hopelessness" that gripped many commentators in the last decades of the Old Regime.[13] Thus this rather typical jeremiad summarizing the year 1768:

> The excessive prices of all things, the irregular morals of people who should rather set an example, the marked infidelity in marriages . . . the corruption in the lower classes, the many bankruptcies, the swarms of tricksters . . . murderers on every streetcorner, attacking people indiscriminately . . . , idleness, mother of vice, producing an infinity of beggars, finally, religion mocked and dishonored in all its dogmas . . . [A]ll of this has filled to the brim the misfortunes of our times, insuring even greater misfortune for our descendants unless heaven, prompted by a general conversion, renders our hearts more obedient to its laws: Fiat, Fiat![14]

Several years later, following a similar litany of crimes and disorders, he exclaimed, echoing a Petrarchan refrain, "Let us close the scene on such horrors and say: O tempora, O Mores!"[15]

Every age has its diehard pessimists, its Jeremiahs; and thus we should resist the temptation to read into Barthès's excoriation of his society and his expressions of despair a premature postmortem of the Old Regime and a moral warrant for the Revolution that would entomb it. Barthès was an opinionated, cranky reactionary, the kind of person for whom the memory of the "good old days" serves as an all-purpose indictment of the present. After a few entries, his catalog of grievances strikes the reader as just about as predictable as Pangloss's cheery refrain.

[13] Simon Schama, *Citizens: A Chronicle of the French Revolution* (New York, 1989), p. 184.
[14] 704:97.
[15] 705:15.

It is, however, worth noting that his denunciations of his contemporaries grew more severe and prolix as the years wore on. Perhaps these were only the grousings of an aging, solitary man who lived to bury three children and two wives, a man increasingly bereft of family and contemporaries. But we should not dismiss the possibility that Barthès's bitter ruminations reflected a real decline in social conditions and public morals, for his criticisms were remarkably scathing, repetitive, and pointed. One recent view of the Old Regime holds that prerevolutionary France was fundamentally sound and healthy and that the Revolution tragically cut short an era committed to the reform of social ills.[16] Though he undoubtedly would have been horrified by the Revolution in all its phases, and likely an early victim of its vengeance as well, there is absolutely no support for this sanguine view of the Old Regime in the pages of his diary. On the contrary, Barthès's criticisms took aim at a whole range of social misfortunes, from high prices to epidemics. Though an enthusiastic supporter of the monarchy's foreign adventures—and something of a xenophobe especially when it came to the English—he bemoaned the social cost of France's various wars, blaming them for much of the misery that surrounded him, wondering out loud at several points when these "ruinous wars" would end. And his normally respectful posture toward the upper classes increasingly gave way to a contempt for their apparent profligacy, which he saw engendering misery for the more modest populace. "The avarice of the great having been so immoderate and so harmful to ordinary people . . . especially poor artisans who have no place to live because of the large population, that everyone is in extreme pain," he observed in 1780.[17] For the first twenty years of the diary his commentary is relatively restrained; then, in 1760, it turns bilious. And after 1770 it becomes downright apocalyptic. That year he despairs of his

[16] Schama, *Citizens.*   [17] 706:36–37.

rhetorical powers, claiming that he "would need a voice stronger than that of the most robust man in order to decry the unfortunate times in which we live and an iron pen to describe the misery, the horrors, and the myriad crimes of the year just ended."[18] In 1771 he exclaims that "the most outrageous hyperbole could not express all the calamities which have touched every family."[19] Two years later his detailed anatomy of contemporary social ills runs to six pages.[20] In 1775 he predicts "even greater misfortunes to come."[21] "How could I describe the horrors and the calamities of the year past?" he asks in 1777.[22] His balance sheet for 1778 combines "all the horrors of every sort of vice that have marked previous years."[23] Having previously doubted his powers of description, in 1779 he proclaims: "I could never cease writing about the horrors of such a year of misfortunes, infinitely greater in cruelties than any other year since the beginning of this century."[24] Finally, in 1780, in one of his last entries, his laconic comment is that "all is going from bad to worse."[25]

Barthès's commentaries show him to be an angry moralizer, a man disgusted with his times, unafraid to vent his spleen on the perceived excesses and crimes of his contemporaries. But as bold as he could be in calumniating his neighbors, both rich and poor, when it came to the authorities, from king to local magistrate and parish priest, he expressed only deference and respect, even awe. He was, in short, the quintessential "little man"—in thrall to the powerful, impatient with the weak, suspicious of change, educated but narrow-minded, convinced that with the erosion of tradition all was lost. Barthès does not tell us why he so dutifully kept his diary, but in recording his observations of city life he was in fact both celebrating tradition, especially the religious rituals and civic

[18] 704:144–46.   [19] 704:170–71.   [20] 705:10–15.
[21] 705:89.   [22] 705:114.   [23] 705:170–71.
[24] 706:12–14.   [25] 706:36–37.

ceremonies that expressed the hierarchical values central to the Old Regime, and documenting with his woeful and vitriolic pen those trends that threatened the world he loved.

Perhaps unwittingly, Barthès's diary reveals something more about his character. As we shall see, he was painstakingly complete in his record of the many public executions staged in Toulouse; indeed, nearly a third of his entries documented the hangings, breakings on the wheel, burnings, brandings, floggings, tortures, and other punishments meted out to a variety of criminals, from murderers and thieves to whores and hapless Huguenots. In one sense, these observations were merely in keeping with his self-imposed obligation to hold up a mirror to all that transpired in his city. But there are few traces of sympathy in his accounts of the atrocious sufferings of the victims, rather a barely disguised relish for the details of their agonies, suggesting a somewhat macabre turn of mind. On one or two occasions he does note that the crowd was moved to pity a young servant girl condemned to hang for the theft of a pittance; or that the stoicism and steadfast faith of a Huguenot minister facing the gallows for illegal proselytizing evoked onlookers' admiration. But Barthès's own commentary reflected his overall identification with the authorities: like them, he viewed the scaffold as the ultimate support of the social order. Thus his callous attitude toward the carnage that passed for criminal justice in the Old Regime. If Barthès occasionally displayed an enthusiasm for executions unbecoming in an official, this only indicates that he was also, in this case at least, a man of the people, who flocked to these events as to a fair. In short, there is no indication that he was affected by the growing belief among many in the eighteenth century that torture and an excessive reliance on capital punishment were both unnecessarily inhumane and ultimately counterproductive aspects of criminal justice. Barthès was a reactionary in this and other respects, but, interestingly, his diary does reveal that humanitarian-minded critics were vocal within his personal milieu. At one point, in 1767, he responds to those "delicate persons" who object to his detailed accounts of executions; in 1776 he concedes that such descriptions may "revolt the reader." Two other asides also reveal an increasing defensiveness about the repetitive entries.[26] But Barthès does not offer a principled justification of his practice, noting that similar accounts can be found in the newspapers of Paris and defiantly adding, in the spirit of *je-m'en-foutisme*: "Read me who wishes, I write for my own pleasure and that should be enough."[27]

THESE brief asides to his critics are virtually the only indication in Barthès's diary that he had readers. But they are significant, giving the lie to his protestations that he wrote simply "for his own pleasure." This in turn opens up the question of the text of "Les heures perdues," not only Barthès's purpose in keeping his diary, but also the development, vicissitudes, and historicity of the diary itself.

Such an interrogation is an essential propaedeutic for Barthès's diary, for we shall be relying exclusively on it for our understanding of public life in eighteenth-century Toulouse. First to consider is its complete title, "Les heures perdues de Pierre Barthès, maître répétiteur en Toulouse, ou recueil des choses digne d'être transmises à la postérité" (The lost hours of Pierre Barthès, master tutor of Toulouse, or a collection of things worthy of being passed down to posterity). Here he specifies at least one audience: not primarily his contemporaries, whom he increasingly viewed with despair, but future generations, who he hoped would be edified by his account. As Carl Becker argued long ago, the eighteenth-century philosophes viewed posterity with a reverence that tended to dis-

[26] 704:11; 705:25–26, 114, 119.   [27] 705:119.

place heaven in their personal cosmologies.[28] Though a firm believer in a celestial aftcrlife, and certainly no philosophe, Barthès seems to have shared their faith in the future; hence the consecration of his diary for the benefit of those readers who would come after him. But he clearly also had contemporary readers, as his several asides indicate. One can only imagine that his diary was passed around among a circle of interested acquaintances—who or how many is a matter of pure speculation.

What of the curious phrase, "The lost hours of Pierre Barthès"? Conveyed here is the image of the casual flaneur, the idle stroller with a penchant for observation, suggesting that his was a less than serious enterprise, merely an assortment of stray notations by a man with time on his hands. Its actual content, however, belies its title, for Barthès is passionate, intensely serious, usually systematic in his detailed observations, and imbued with a mission to document both the splendors and the miseries of his age. Like the inclusion of the dream at the start of the diary, the title bespeaks an initial intent quickly undermined by the text itself.

Barthès was certainly not the first chronicler of Toulouse's public life. In fact, his diary owes its inspiration largely to a previous memoir from the end of Louis XIV's reign, a manuscript that has not survived which Barthès mentions having consulted.[29] It is possible too that he was aware of another journal kept by a Toulousain, this one by the merchant Elie Esquirol, whose brief account of public events between 1596 and 1632 is, however, quite bereft of both detail and interest.[30] The most authoritative chronicle of city life was the official

[28] Carl L. Becker, *The Heavenly City of the Eighteenth-Century Philosophers* (New Haven and London, 1932).

[29] 705:177.

[30] "Journal d'Elie Esquirol, marchand de Toulouse (1596–1632)," Bibliothèque nationale, fonds français, nouvelles acquisitions: 22255, fol. 472.

record kept by the town councillors, or *capitouls*, of Toulouse, drawn up at the end of each year from the early sixteenth century to the Revolution. The eleven tomes constituting the "Annales manuscrits de la Ville de Toulouse" are an invaluable source on the city's history, read by every local historian both past and present.[31] Barthès several times mentions consulting them.[32] Indeed, one might speculate that he saw his own journal as a supplement to the official "Annales," for a comparison between the capitouls' accounts in the eighteenth century and those from previous times reveals a striking decline in detail and comprehensiveness as the Old Regime waned—a decline in keeping with the waning power and vitality of municipal government.

Beyond these manuscript chronicles there were several printed histories of Toulouse available to Barthès. Two date from the sixteenth century, Nicolas Bertrandi's *Les gestes de tholosans*, first published in Latin in 1515, and *Histoire tolosain* (1555) by Antoine Noguier, both mixtures of fact and fable. Barthès refers to Bertrandi and cites as well Guillaume de Catel's more dependable *Mémoire de l'histoire de Languedoc* (1633), devoted, in part, to the history and description of the city of Toulouse.[33] He also cites Germain de Lafaille, the municipal syndic, whose two-volume *Annales de la Ville de Toulouse* (1682 and 1701), a year-by-year summary of local events beginning in the thirteenth century, was based on the capitouls' "Annales" and other documents deposited in the archives of the Hôtel de Ville.[34] In 1776 Barnabé de Rosoi, a minor *philosophe*, contributed his four-tome history of Toulouse, a work similar to Lafaille's in scope and design but infused with the spirit of the Enlightenment. Barthès, a local

[31] Bibliothèque municipale de Toulouse, BB 274–84.
[32] See, for example, 700:48.
[33] 703:185, 700:48.
[34] 700:50.

savant and a man steeped in the history of his city, was likely familiar with this work. He was definitely familiar with Jean Raynal's *Histoire de Toulouse* (1759), another local history influenced by the critical spirit of the age.[35] But "Les heures perdues" differs fundamentally from these previous histories of Toulouse. It belongs instead to the genre of descriptions of cities, found in guidebooks, almanacs, memoirs, and the like, which became popular especially in the eighteenth century.[36] Like these accounts, Barthès's diary eschews history for a description of contemporary city life in its variety and plenitude. The two undisputed masters of the genre who raised it to a literary art form were Sebastian Mercier and Restif de la Bretonne, who trained their eyes on Parisian life, both high and low. In the preface to his *Tableau de Paris*, published in 1782 just two years after Barthès's diary breaks off, Mercier argues for the virtue of observing "what is before our eyes" rather than "useless" preoccupation with the "dead past."[37] Barthès did not express any such disdain for the study of history, but, like Mercier, although of course on a much lower literary level, he kept his vision fixed on the stuff of daily life in his city. And unlike either Mercier or Restif, he shunned communing with the seamy side of his city except to express his moral disapprobation at a distance, displaying virtually a willful blindness to the rich world of popular pastimes and rituals. It was thus more than inferior literary artistry that separated Barthès from these Parisian men of letters— it was a lack of intellectual curiosity compounded by moral priggishness.

But what Barthès lacked he at least partially compensated for with a quality rarely displayed by more cosmopolitan ob-

---

[35] 703:65.

[36] On these see Robert Darnton, "A Bourgeois Puts His World in Order: The City as Text," in *The Great Cat Massacre and Other Episodes in French Cultural History* (New York, 1984), pp. 107–43.

[37] L.-S. Mercier, *Tableau de Paris*, 12 vols. (Amsterdam, 1782–1786), 1:xi.

servers of Paris: a passionate commitment to his city that marked him as a municipal patriot. Barthès was part of an intellectual movement apparent in the latter half of the eighteenth century that signaled a revived interest in provincial life on the part of locals after several generations in submission to the ways and preoccupations of Paris.[38] And in this sense, his enterprise shares something of the spirit that motivated another contemporary, an anonymous "bourgeois" of nearby Montpellier, to assemble an exhaustive portrait of his city: its buildings and monuments, the many ceremonies and amusements that marked public life, its variety of inhabitants, their occupations, and what we would call their life-styles.[39] Barthès's diary was less systematic than the Montpelliérain's long-winded description and favored a chronological survey focusing on ceremony over an anatomy of the urban order and cityscape. But the two observers were alike in a moralizing tone that marks their texts, as well as a deeply held municipal patriotism that clearly motivated them. And neither of their texts found its way into print.

In an age of print, this fact is worth pondering. In Barthès's case, however, it was not for want of trying. In fact, there is evidence that he aspired to the status of *auteur*. During the first year of its publication, his accounts were included, sometimes verbatim but always anonymously, in the earliest newspaper of Toulouse, the *Annonces, affiches et avis divers*.[40] But

[38] Daniel Roche, *Les républicains des lettres* (Paris, 1988), pp. 194–99. If I had been more sensitive to the "provincialism" that Roche convincingly argues played an important role in the intellectual life of French cities, including Toulouse, I might have qualified my conclusion regarding the cosmopolitan cast of elite culture in eighteenth-century Toulouse in my book *Public Life in Toulouse*.

[39] Published by Joseph Berthelé, "Montpellier en 1768 d'après un manuscrit anonyme inédit," in *Archives de la ville de Montpellier* (Montpellier, 1909), vol. 4; see Darnton, "A Bourgeois Puts His World in Order," in *The Great Cat Massacre*.

[40] *Annonces, affiches et avis divers*, June 12, 1759–January 8, 1760. I owe

after its editorial control changed hands in 1760, the pages of the *Annonces* were closed to his contributions. He faithfully continued to record his observations nevertheless, with little hope of publication. Thus, his unprinted diary reminds us that even in the eighteenth century there persisted a culture of script removed from the world of print, that a literature could circulate outside the book trade, for we know that "Les heures perdues" had contemporary readers. It demonstrates as well that the passage from script to print could work both ways: Barthès copies whole articles from the *Gazette de France* into his journal, padding his pages with what were, after all, handwritten transcriptions of readily available printed accounts entirely unrelated to Toulouse. Usually these entries concern events such as the death of a foreign monarch or a significant contemporary catastrophe like the Lisbon earthquake or the great fire in Cairo. (Although in addition he displayed a persistent fascination with human longevity, citing scores of notable cases from far and wide: in April 1753, for example, he announced the death of the "oldest of all men," a gentleman from Worcester who died at the age of 130.)[41] Barthès's text also suggests that the diary form, often considered emblematic of a deepening divide between public and private spheres in the eighteenth century, could be quintessentially public in nature.

The manuscript form of "Les heures perdues" also highlights what we might call, for want of a better term, its rustic quality. If Barthès had been a villager and trained his eye on the ceremonies, rituals, and pastimes of peasants, we would

---

this information to Professor Michel Taillefer of the University of Toulouse-Mirail.

[41] 701:35. Although later he noted the death of a Scotsman of 132 years but could not resist a dig at his religion: "The old age of this man whom I call the patriarch of Protestants would have been a thousand times happier if he had more solid principles and more orthodox beliefs." 702:116.

have no trouble classifying him as a folklorist, a sort of early ethnographer. But his was an urban milieu, his natives city-dwellers, and his interest largely in official, not popular, life. Barthès's bigotry, his manifest disdain for the populace, and his deference to the authorities would seem to distinguish him from those collectors of popular practices whose labors amounted to what Peter Burke has called "the discovery of the people" in late-eighteenth-century Europe.[42] And yet he was a scrupulous observer of daily life, albeit his curiosity did remain limited to Toulouse's major thoroughfares and plazas, never straying to its back alleys or more obscure haunts. Perhaps the best way to describe Barthès is indeed as a municipal patriot, a sort of civic booster, whose identification with his city and its official life led him to record those events, both momentous and routine, that marked the city as a special environment in an overwhelmingly rural society. His patriotism was not merely passive, for, as noted, he frequently contributed to civic festivities as a deviser of Latin inscriptions. In a supposedly cosmopolitan age, Barthès's world was still defined by his city, his passions those of a man enthralled with the day-to-day drama in this provincial urban milieu.

It is a curious feature of social history that we know less about this milieu than we do either of elites or of the laboring classes.[43] Even the urban poor have received more scholarly attention than the world of the provincial literate. Barthès himself does not seem to fit into our ready-made categories for describing the social and cultural order of the Old Regime. He was not of the Enlightenment—not an academician or Free-mason; not a member of the ecclesiastical establishment; not an official or craftsman belonging to the city's corporate hierarchy; not a merchant or tradesman; and certainly not, despite his humble origins, a man of the people, whose credulity and

---

[42] Burke, *Popular Culture*, pp. 3–22.
[43] The exception being the work of Daniel Roche.

dissoluteness he condemned at every turn. How to classify him? We might borrow the categories used by Robert Redfield in his *The Primitive World and Its Transformations*. Redfield suggests a distinction between the "literati," the literate and educated in simple societies who serve as defenders of indigenous traditions and interpreters of usually aristocratic social and cultural forms; and the "intelligentsia," those bearers of cosmopolitan, usually intrusive values that challenge provincial, traditional ways.[44] In these terms, Barthès was certainly a member of the literati, indeed, an enemy of the intelligentsia, as his ceaseless celebrations of both the established order and traditional Catholicity bear out. In Barthès's particular case, however, his identification with the city and its glories can perhaps be explained as well by his professional activities as a tutor of Latin. His diary, after all, demonstrates a familiarity with those classical authors, especially Cicero, who wrote in praise of the active life in service to the city, and whose writings were essential to the birth of civic humanism in the fifteenth century. Though he probably did not need an intellectual justification for his municipal patriotism, Barthès certainly could have found ample inspiration for his fierce local sentiments in the texts he read, taught, and committed to memory.

Barthès was a man of learning, if not erudition or profound thought. And from his diary, we can easily reconstruct a sample of his reading diet, as well as point out some features of his mental makeup. Not surprisingly, the texts he seems most comfortable with were those classical authors who formed the basis of the college *studium*: Cicero, Horace, Virgil, Seneca, and Ovid. These are the sources of most of his Latin quota-

[44] Robert Redfield, *The Primitive World and Its Transformations* (Ithaca, 1967 ed.), pp. 43–44. See also the comments of Inga Clendinnen, *Ambivalent Conquests: Maya and Spaniard in Yucatan, 1517–1570* (Cambridge, 1987), p. 185.

tions, which are also interlaced with biblical citations in Latin, especially from the Psalms. As noted, he was a faithful reader of the *Gazette de France*, a source of many of his entries. But this rather cosmopolitan reading diet was balanced by more local fare—the various histories of Toulouse, both printed and in manuscript. These are the texts he cites most readily, and it is clear that they are his constant companions as he strives to relate the present-day life of his city to its past.

The appearance of a comet in the skies over Toulouse in January 1744 serves as an occasion for Barthès to demonstrate his familiarity with scientific matters, as well as his desire to present an accurate account in the face of wrongheaded popular beliefs. In fact, he interrupts his account of the extraordinary phenomenon, pausing in the diary after its appearance, only to return to the matter several days later, presumably having consulted what astronomical texts he had at his disposal. As someone respectful of learning, he clearly wanted to get things right. What he comes up with, however, is a half-accurate, somewhat garbled version of scientific opinion a generation earlier. In his long-winded discourse he concludes that comets were the product of the earth's exhalations or vapors, an approximate, though fundamentally incorrect, version of the late-seventeenth-century view that they were produced by other heavenly bodies. But with equal certitude he also observes them to be both signs and causes of war, revolts, drought, plague, earthquakes, and the "death of potentates"— this from a man who bemoaned, in this case and others, the rampant superstition among the common people.[45]

There is another interesting facet of Barthès's literary or, more precisely, linguistic proclivities—one not to be found in his diary, however. Not a word of "Les heures perdues" is written in Occitan; it betrays no hint that Barthès spoke "la len-

---

[45] 699:131, 134–39. For contemporary views of the nature of comets, see "Comète," *Encyclopédie ou Dictionnaire raisonné des sciences, des arts, et des métiers* (1778 edition), vol. 8, pt. 2, pp. 583–99.

gua mondina," Toulouse's own patois. Given his disdain for things popular, one might assume that he would have considered such a talent beneath him. And yet he did compose several poems in Occitan that were printed in the first editions of the *Annonces, affiches et avis divers.*[46] The son of an artisan, he most certainly spoke Occitan growing up. But these poems were not rustic scribblings, nor did they even preserve the oral quality of Occitan. They were rather composed as part of a game in which an "enigmatic" word was proposed by the editor and readers were invited to submit verses explaining it in artful, witty terms. By participating in this game, Barthès was making a public display of his literary talents; by submitting verses in *Occitan*, he was showing his colors as a literary person who had not lost his local pride.

Barthès's diary reads as a continuous testimony to this pride, and especially to his conviction that the ceremonial life of his city was worth recording, even celebrating. Celebrated, however, are not only the religious and political institutions that gave rise to ceremonial expression—the Christian faith and reverence for the monarchy central to his worldview—but perhaps more profoundly the idea of an orderly, hierarchically configured world. Barthès the man believed in order: hence his celebration of the orderly city ceremonially represented. But Barthès's *text* displays a perhaps unwanted contradiction between order and disorder. Ceremonial representations of order compete for space with the "disorderly" intrusions of poverty, rioting, crime, irreverence, and political conflict in the pages of "Les heures perdues." And it was these intrusions that led to the mounting despair which characterized his observations. One might speculate that Barthès began his enterprise with the intent of celebrating his orderly city but found himself increasingly obliged to acknowledge the disorder that

---

[46] Michel Taillefer, "Pierre Barthès, Rimeur Occitan," *L'Auta*, n.s., no. 500 (November 1984): 259–66. I am again grateful to Professor Taillefer for sharing this article with me.

blighted his view. If so, this would explain, among other things, his proclivity for describing executions, for it was on the scaffold that the "disorder" of crime was effaced in the orderly ritual of public death.

How to summarize such a man? One would think the task easy. He was, after all, neither endowed with unique intelligence or psychological complexity, nor burdened with the travails and vicissitudes of wielding power in public life. One might even characterize him as typical, a sort of eighteenth-century Everyman, insofar as he echoed, often platitudinously, the dominant values and outlook of his times. And yet what is supposedly typical can still resist characterization, and thus, ultimately, comprehension. To resort to anachronisms—reactionary, bigot—(a historical sin that unfortunately I have not successfully avoided here), is not terribly helpful. But one label—this too something of an anachronism—would seem to be appropriate. Barthès was deeply conservative; indeed, a catalog of his most salient values and principles would seem to amount to a conservative checklist. First, he continuously expressed respect and admiration, even awe, for men of power and office; for him the hierarchy was sacred. Second, he saw himself as a moral guardian, defending the church against unbelievers and cynics, bewailing the depravity of public comportment, and generally voicing despair at the evidence of moral decline he saw everywhere. Finally, his ceaseless attacks on the growing penchant for luxury among rich and modest alike, the most pointed among his criticisms, marked his conservatism as rooted in the contemporary view that excess wealth and material prodigality were both signs and causes of corruption.

As a conservative, Barthès differed from other eighteenth-century writers known to us whose origins were likewise plebian. Restif de la Bretonne was a freethinker; Jacques-Louis

Ménétra, a boastful libertine; and Jamerey-Duval, something of a philosopher, or at least a wide-ranging critic. Even the scribe Pierre Prion, whose modern-day editors characterize as "conservative," espoused a Copernican cosmology and voiced, albeit in muted tones, anticlerical and antiseignorial views.[47] Compared to these men, Barthès was the model of conventionality (as well as mediocrity: he ranked far beneath them in terms of literary originality and ambition). And yet his penchant for persistent, sometimes scathing, criticism cannot be ignored as merely a feature of his outraged conservatism.

I would suggest, rather, that he was something of a Christian humanist, a label not usually employed in the context of the eighteenth century, but justified in the case of a man whose worldview was so marked by a combination of traditionalism, piety, pretense to learning, and criticism, and among whose most precious attachments ranked the Society of Jesus. Two aspects of his value system are worth reiterating to make this case. First was his criticism of the frequently bizarre beliefs and behavior of ordinary people, whom Barthès railed against as benighted and vulgar. To choose but one example: when the site of the exposed bodies of artisans executed following riots in 1747 turned into a pilgrimage spot for legions of Toulousains convinced that the corpses possessed miraculous properties, he unleashed a diatribe against "this ignorant and credulous people, this many-headed beast, fickle and rudderless."[48] A condescending, despairing attitude toward the intellectual capacities of the lower classes ranked among the features of the Enlightenment, of course, but it also harked back to the earlier humanists. Second, his repeated

[47] Emmanuel Le Roy Ladurie and Orest Ranum, eds., *Pierre Prion, scribe: mémoires d'un écrivain de campagne au XVIIIe siècle* (Paris, 1985), p. 33. The editors of this volume compare and characterize these various plebian writers.
[48] 699:267.

criticism of the materialism and lust for luxuries of his neighbors put him in league with a large band of contemporary
moralists—Catholics, physiocrats, Rousseauists, civic republi-
cans, future Jacobins—but with the tradition of Christian humanism as well. It is noteworthy that he also bemoaned, not
simply luxury, but both the growing divide between rich and
poor and the deleterious effects of "avarice" and profligacy of
the wealthy on the modest and indigent. I would suggest,
therefore, that what we have in Barthès is not simply a tradi-
tionalist or a conservative, but someone who, while standing
outside the Enlightenment, still partook of the critical, moralizing spirit of the day. That we think of this spirit in the
eighteenth century largely in terms of the Enlightenment
means that we exclude from our view other traditions, such as
Christian humanism, which while no longer novel still could
exert a considerable influence over the minds of the educated.[49] And we also risk underestimating and mischaracter-
izing provincial literati such as Pierre Barthès—our guide to
eighteenth-century Toulouse.

[49] On the continued strength of the traditional and humanistic values in
university circles in the eighteenth century, see L.W.B. Brockliss, *French
Higher Education in the Seventeenth and Eighteenth Centuries: A Cultural
History* (Oxford, 1987).

CHAPTER 2

THE CITY

Troops in Toulouse

The first of this month at four in the afternoon arrived in Toulouse by the Porte de Château the Regiment Gantes Volontaires, composed of three companies of infantry, one of horse-mounted Dragoons. [. . .] They were lodged in the faubourg of Saint-Michel and the Saint-Cyprien quartier in the homes of some bourgeois (something unheard-of), because Toulouse has never seen these sorts of men inside its gates. The guards were established in the new house of M. Coudère, formerly a notary, the officers in the homes of notables of the quartier, and the others in different homes by lot. . . .

"Les heures perdues," January 1748 (699:257)

In the beginning of this month, demolition was started on a block of very poorly constructed houses located on one side of the small Place du Salin across from the Hôtel des monnoies. This plaza, extremely irregular in form because of the handful of very poorly constructed buildings, will soon be one of the most pleasant spots in the city and will very nicely dress up the entry to the [parlement's] palace and that of the Hôtel des

monnoies, for which one now has to search and which most
visitors are unaware of, enclosed as it is at the point of two
ugly little streets that meet there and totally block the view.

"Les heures perdues," April 1754 (702:5)

B ARTHÈS'S CITY was an administrative capital for much of southwestern France, thus the stage for the myriad official displays and ceremonies that fill his diary. Indeed, since the eclipse in the mid-sixteenth century of its pastel industry, which had briefly transformed the city into a commercial capital of continental importance, Toulouse remained for the most part a provincial center for a range of ecclesiastical and secular institutions. The institution that ensured its administrative centrality was the Parlement of Toulouse, a body of over one hundred Robe noblemen of imposing wealth and collective power. There were other royal courts in the city: the présidial, the sénéchal, as well as several minor adjudicating bodies, together spawning a substantial community of lawyers, barristers, notaries, scribes, and other legal functionaries who served the courts. Many of these lawmen were educated at the University of Toulouse, founded in the thirteenth century, a major center for the study of civil law. Although somewhat in decline from its preeminence in the sixteenth century, when Toulouse was one of the two cities in the realm where the teaching of Roman law was permitted, the university still attracted a substantial number of students from throughout France and western Europe.

Toulouse's many magistrates and lawmen, its royal and local officialdom, rubbed shoulders—and sometimes jockeyed for position—with a large and varied ecclesiastical community, from church hierarchs, such as the archbishop and the canons of the Cathedral Saint-Etienne and the Basilica Saint-Sernin, to the scores of parish priests and regular clergy who ministered to the faithful. The city was dense with religious institutions—parish churches, penitential chapels, monasteries, colleges, hospitals, ecclesiastical courts, devotional confraternities, and even the Dominican office of the Inquisition of the Faith, a relic of the thirteenth century. Not a day passed when at least one of these bodies did not take to the streets in procession or other devotional ritual, and Barthès was often there to record the event.

If its myriad legal and ecclesiastical bodies gave Toulouse a hierarchical, official, somewhat conservative tone, this was only highlighted by its lack of economic vitality. To be sure, the city had a substantial and varied population of merchants, tradesmen, and artisans, most of whom catered to the consumption needs of magistrates' households and religious communities. As well, Toulouse had long been a regional entrepôt for the rich grain-growing lands that lie east of the city; and with the construction of the Canal du Midi in the late seventeenth century, the city provided an essential link in the Mediterranean grain trade. But a great commercial or industrial center it was not. Unlike France's Atlantic seaboard cities, whose prosperity increased with the rise in American trade, or such industrial towns as Lille, Rouen, or Grenoble, or even its provincial rival Montpellier, a hive of economic activity, Toulouse's economy remained traditional—guild-bound, preindustrial, and local, typical for such an administrative center. One result of its economic languor was that the city experienced only a modest population increase over the course of the eighteenth century, less, proportionally, than France as a whole, and was significantly outpaced demographically by several other cities. While in the sixteenth century, with a population of 40,000, it ranked second among France's cities, by the prerevolutionary era, with 53,000 inhabitants, it had slipped to ninth place.[1] Much of that comparatively moderate increase was made up of immigrants from the surrounding countryside: one researcher has calculated that in the century

[1] On population figures for Toulouse and other French cities, see Philip Benedict, "French Cities from the Sixteenth Century to the Revolution: An Overview," in *Cities and Social Change in Early Modern France*, ed. Benedict (London, 1989), and Roger Chartier et al., *La ville classique: de la Renaissance aux Revolutions*, vol. 3 of *Histoire de la France urbaine*, ed. Georges Duby (Paris, 1981), p. 297.

before the Revolution, over 37,000 migrants found their way to Toulouse.[2] Some of these migrants were craftsmen and workers drawn to the provincial capital to labor on several new public building projects. Many, if not most, were rural indigents seeking sustenance in the big city. Thus, far beneath the judicial and ecclesiastical hierarchy that dominated the social order, and below the merchant and craft community that serviced the developing consumer economy, was a growing, often turbulent population of poor people. Eighteenth-century Toulouse was not unique among French cities in being burdened with an underclass of indigents. The swelling of the ranks of the poor, especially from the immiserization and itinerancy that accompanied the uprooting of peasants from their lands, was a salient feature of prerevolutionary France. A large portion of these rural vagabonds made their way to cities, hoping to find work or public charity, but were often forced to resort to begging, prostitution, or theft.

Barthès's diary documents, although in purely impressionistic and personal terms, the crushing presence of the poor in eighteenth-century Toulouse, as well as some of the measures the authorities took to deal with them. His own attitude toward indigency was severe, lacking in that Christian charity one would expect from such a fervent believer. He does acknowledge that many honorable and hardworking families blamelessly sank into poverty as prices rose precipitously and unemployment spread, and even concedes, with slight sympathy, that grain rioters were motivated in part by misery, not only by lawlessness. But in general he viewed the poor, especially the many foreign mendicants, as a "mass of tricksters and vagabonds" who threatened the public order with their aggressive, often criminal, behavior. In his terms the city was

---

[2] Jean Coppolani, *Toulouse: étude de géographie urbaine* (Toulouse, 1954), p. 103. See also Schneider, *Public Life in Toulouse*, pp. 33–34.

"overwhelmed," "flooded," by an "abundance of good-for-nothings," "swarming" with brigands disguised as beggars—those primarily responsible for the growing number of thefts and assaults he repeatedly decried in his diary. Barthès was a spokesman for the Toulouse of property and privilege, despite his humble status; hence his readiness to view the poor as a menacing, fearful presence. According to him, the city was under siege, constantly threatened by "strangers and disreputable characters who . . . under the pretext of begging . . . force their way into people's homes in broad daylight, holding them hostage with a pistol to their throats."[3] Hence too his enthusiastic approval of the periodic attempts to police the poor. On at least ten occasions, from 1738 to 1780, the capitouls ordered the expulsion from the city of all the "foreign" poor—that is to say, those not of Toulouse.[4] In 1739, the city offered the opportunity of work on a new quay as an alternative to expulsion, an offer that five hundred indigents accepted for three sols a day. A note of poignancy creeps into Barthès's account when he notes that whole families, including children of three or four, could be seen among the laborers.[5] On Christmas Eve 1751, over three thousand needy men, women, and children enlisted in a similar public works project.[6] In 1765, along with expelling the foreign poor, the capitouls equipped resident indigents with tin badges inscribed with the city's emblem and a number to facilitate an orderly and just distribution of alms.[7] Despite these and other public efforts, urban poverty and mendicancy continued unabated, furnishing Barthès with a constant source of complaint.

His complaint, however, was not limited to the poor. Much has been written about the emergence of a consumer

[3] 703:200.
[4] 699:13, 41–42; 234–35; 700:11; 702:14–15; 703:171, 182, 199–200; 705:10. In March of 1776 the city's prostitutes were also expelled: 705:94–95.
[5] 699:41–42   [6] 700:39–41.   [7] 703:200.

economy in France and elsewhere in the eighteenth century—
the economic development that placed a variety of consum-
ables and luxury goods within the purchasing reach of a wider
range of people and the expanded commercial enterprises that
catered to this larger consuming populace, especially in cities.[8]
Barthès witnessed the local development of this consumer
economy, but, as noted, he was uncompromisingly critical in
his observations. He saw nothing to celebrate in his neighbors'
pursuit of luxuries, for they were, in his words, merely "tyran-
nized by fashion." Even "the most rustic peasant and his wife
were agitated by the same vertiginous spirit"—"the same luxury that I call the decay of the human spirit."[9] Not surprisingly, given the prevalent misogyny he shared, he viewed
women as most vulnerable to the demands of fashion, "which
change each day with a swiftness that hardly gives one twenty-
four hours to keep up, so much has luxury prevailed, dragging
women into the most degraded state."[10] Fashion was responsible for a multitude of evils: "disorderliness" among women
and girls, a decline in public morality, the "confusion" of social ranks, indebtedness, and the proliferation of bankruptcies.
His condemnation takes on a Rousseauist tone, as when he
denounces the "baneful insolence of women, ruined by luxury, who in the streets, the theaters, and even in church auda-
ciously insult the simple dress of honest citizens."[11] And,
somewhat surprisingly, he is even willing to draw a causal con-
nection between the profligacy, "avarice," and "outrageous
luxury" of the rich and the widening misery of much of the
populace.

[8] See, for example, Daniel Roche, *Le peuple de Paris* (Paris, 1981), chap.
5; Annik Pardailhé-Galabrun, *The Birth of Intimacy: Privacy and Domestic
Life in Early Modern Paris*, trans. Jocelyn Phelps (Philadelphia, 1991); and
James R. Farr, "Consumers, Commerce, and the Craftsmen of Dijon: The
Changing Social and Economic Structure of a Provincial Capital, 1450–
1750," in Benedict, *Cities and Social Change*, pp. 134–73.
[9] 703:150; 704:144–45. [10] 705:145. [11] 704:40–41.

Beneath the moralizing, opinionated commentary of Barthès, therefore, one finds an accurate, if unsophisticated, social analysis of an eighteenth-century city. It is a city increasingly divided between the well-provided and the poor, with the ranks of the latter expanding steadily. It is also a society in which increasing wealth and greater market opportunities prompted a tendency toward conspicuous consumption, thus challenging some traditional expectations—Barthès's, for example—of how people should behave.

If Barthès looked upon such changes disapprovingly, he viewed other transformations in his city with a more favorable eye. While socially eighteenth-century Toulouse seemed blighted by poverty and crime, physically it was taking on a new and more attractive face. The spirit of urbanism was at work, effecting renovations, new construction, and clearing projects that went a long way in transforming the still medieval city into a modern metropolis. Not since the sixteenth century, when the wealth garnered from the pastel industry promoted the construction of scores of private hôtels, had Toulouse experienced such a flurry of architectural activity, most of it documented by Barthès with a pride befitting a true civic booster. He notes the removal of many of the city's crosses, once emblematic of the populace's piety, now considered a hindrance to traffic; the elevation of a neoclassical facade for the Hôtel de Ville; the construction of a series of esplanades, promenades, and quays along the Garonne River; the clearing and refurbishing of both the Place Saint-Mage and the Place du Pont Neuf; the repair of an aqueduct in the quartier of the Dalbade; the inauguration of a new fountain in the Place Saint-Etienne; the reopening and modernizing of several markets; the entire demolition and reconstruction of the parish church of the Daurade; the construction of the Canal Brienne; and the clearing of the Place Royale, the large plaza in front of the city hall, of shops and other commercial establishments. Most of these projects met with Barthès's approval, especially those such as the face-lifting and embellishment of the Hôtel de Ville where his skill as a Latinist was called into service. (He composed the inscriptions etched into the facade.)[12] But his conservative temperament sometimes balked at the wholesale destruction that some of these enterprises entailed. He bemoaned, for example, the demolition of houses required to construct the Cour Dillon, an esplanade on the Garonne's left bank.[13] Ever concerned with public morality, he pronounced that it would only attract "good-for-nothings intent on wasting their time wandering and indulging in frivolous pleasures."

Such new constructions and renovations ranked among the cherished innovations in eighteenth-century Toulouse— proudly displayed to visiting dignitaries by municipal officials and commented upon by our diarist at length. There was another innovation that drew less favorable comment. In 1748, following a tumultuous grain riot lasting several days, royal troops occupied the city. Like most cities, Toulouse regarded the right to be spared the quartering and billeting of troops as a fundamental privilege, which had been respected, with isolated exceptions, throughout the Old Regime. In the second half of the eighteenth century, however, this right was regularly violated, with royal troops becoming a near-permanent fixture on the local scene. The arrival of the regiment Gantes Volontaires in January 1748 was only the first of a series of military visitations, all noted by Barthès. He did not disapprove of this move, for, like the authorities, he recognized the need for increased armed security in the face of popular unrest; but he did object to the fact that some of the troops were quartered "chez les bourgeois."[14] And his irritation is evident

---

[12] 700:54; 702:54, 62, 143, 148, 152, 150, 171; 703:152; 704:19–22, 46, 95–96, 104–5, 148; 705:126, 151–52, 179.
[13] 703:187.   [14] 699:294.

when he recounts that residents and tradesmen were expelled from their houses and shops in order to allow for the posting of armed guards in the city's squares.[15]

Barthès documents the comings and goings of troops over the years, offering a comment now and again on their comportment, size, and martial bearing. He describes both the military parades and mock deployments that delighted the populace and the many firing squads that were the fate of military deserters. Sometimes a regiment would arrive in town in a festive fanfare reminiscent of a ritual entry; on other occasions, such as when the parlement refused to register the royal edict for the *vingtième* (a new tax), the troops stealthily moved in as an occupying force. In any case, the procession of military men confronted the populace with a strange and not always reassuring presence in its midst. Altercations between troops and townsfolk were frequent; so too were sexual liaisons, sometimes resulting in savage punishment for the implicated women (see below, chapter 3). In 1748 Barthès echoes an apparently widespread complaint that the soldiers of the Gantes Volontaires "daily insult great and small alike and seize anything they can get their hands on."[16] But he notes in 1774 that the Regiment Alsace-Allemand was composed of mostly well-behaved men who, however, "seemed to come from the Antipodes. No one understood their language." Though capable only of "speaking through signs like the Iroquois," they nonetheless made "several conquests" in the neighborhood where they were lodged.[17] From "Les heures perdues" we can assemble a table listing the passage of troops in Toulouse from their introduction in 1748 (see table 1).

With the regular presence of royal troops in the city, Toulouse was subjected to a greater range and depth of armed might than ever before in its history. There were in fact three components of this armed might. The first was the traditional

[15] 699:302–3, 321–22.   [16] 699:262.   [17] 705:16, 29.

THE CITY

TABLE 1
Royal Troops in Toulouse, 1738–1780

Regiment	Date of Arrival	Length of Stay
Gantes Volontaires	Jan. 1, 1748	4½ months
Milices du Perigord	Jan. 3, 1748	5 months
Bourbonnais	Feb. 14, 1749	18 months
Vieille Marine	Aug. 3, 1750	13 months
Quercy	Oct. 5, 1751	10 months
Bresse	Oct. 7, 1751	10 months
de la Reine	Nov. 3, 1752	50 days
Anjou	Oct. 15, 1753	16 months
de la Sarre	Feb. 26, 1755	1 year
Traisnel	Aug. 22, 1756	7 months
Roche-Aymon	June 28, 1760	9 months
Berry	March 16, 1761	1 month
Montmorin	May 1761	2 days
Berry	July 6, 1761	10 months
Béarn	July 8, 1761	10 months
de la Sarre	Aug. 8, 1761	?
Royal-Vaisseaux	Sept. 9, 1763	5½ months
Cavalerie du Roy	Sept. 20, 1763	5½ months
Hainaut	Nov. 18, 1763	44 days
Cavalerie du Roy	Oct. 1764	5 months
Royal-Perigord	Apr. 26, 1773	?
Alsace-Allemand	Jan. 28, 1774	7 months

corps of city militiamen, the Guet or Watch, whose size was more than doubled in the course of the century and whose power was augmented with carbines and bayonets.[18] The second were the royal troops who frequently patrolled the city, sometimes accompanied by the capitouls.[19] Like these royal troops, the third component also came from outside the city.

[18] Schneider, *Public Life in Toulouse*, p. 319, and sources cited.
[19] 699:317.

Increasingly after its reform in the earlier part of the century, the *maréchaussée*, or royal constabulary, began to appear regularly on the local scene. For example, in May 1740 these mounted troops entered the city escorting a group of criminals for trial before the parlement.[20] Two years later it was they, not the Watch, who were charged with the task of expelling all the indigent beggars from the city.[21] They also became a fixture in the city's ceremonial life, appearing prominently in the ritual entries that greeted visiting dignitaries and in other displays.[22] And they frequently participated in public executions, surrounding the scaffold in a protective cordon against possible crowd violence. Much has been made of the small size of the maréchaussée, whose few numbers, something like four thousand, have struck historians as pitifully meager for a police force for the realm's entire countryside.[23] Even so, their near-permanent presence in eighteenth-century Toulouse, coupled with an augmented Guet and royal troops, amounted to an impresssive and menacing show of force. Like the forced submission of municipal government to the control of the intendant at the end of the seventeenth century, the presence of these outside armed forces, both the maréchaussée and royal troops, signaled the further erosion of Toulouse's independence and autonomy in the face of royal interference.

FROM THE perspective of the long run of the Old Regime, nothing epitomizes the distinctiveness of the eighteenth century more than this military presence in Toulouse—the city

[20] 699:59–60.

[21] 699:99.

[22] For example, 699:57; 702:129–30.

[23] On the maréchaussée, see Olwen Hufton, *The Poor of Eighteenth-Century France, 1750–1789* (Oxford, 1974); Robert Schwartz, *Policing the Poor in Eighteenth-Century France* (Chapel Hill, 1988); and Iain A. Cameron, *Crime and Repression in the Auvergne and the Guyenne, 1720–1790* (Cambridge, 1981).

that once proudly called itself a "municipal republic."[24] Indeed, much that Barthès presents us highlights what was particular to his times: the mounting indigency against a backdrop of conspicuous luxury and consumerism, the new urbanism that began physically to transform the city, as well as the novel ceremonial forms that we shall investigate in future chapters. But much in his diary also reminds us of what was constant about the early modern urban experience, especially the natural and man-made disasters that regularly afflicted the city. We are accustomed to viewing the city as a privileged environment, protected behind its walls, in some ways sheltered from the elements. "Les heures perdues" vividly shows us how precarious urban life could be, even in the eighteenth century.

People were not even safe in their own homes, for buildings collapsed, roofs caved in, foundations gave way, and walls crumbled with some regularity. Sometimes these mishaps were caused by lightning or violent storms; especially vulnerable were houses located close to the Garonne's banks, where years of constant flooding undermined their foundations. Barthès records nearly thirty such structural disasters, some causing fatalities. One notable accident occurred during mass at the church of the Dalbade in June 1752. Just as the priest was pronouncing the benediction, a loud cracking noise was heard overhead accompanied by some dust cascading from the ceiling around the organ. Panic broke out among the assembled, who were convinced that the church's ceiling was collapsing, and in the ensuing stampede scores were injured, many carried out half-dead. The tragic event had a ludicrous cause: it seems that during the service the organist became enraged at his assistant, who had refused to fetch a lantern, and hurled a chair at him, thus loosening several planks in the church's

[24] Schneider, *Public Life in Toulouse*, pt. 1.

loft.[25] Ten years later, a bridge over the fishmarket on the Island of Tounis collapsed, causing much injury and extensive destruction.[26] Just as frequent were fires, a particularly dreaded disaster for the city of Toulouse, which was nearly destroyed by raging flames in 1463. The eighteenth century was spared such a conflagration, probably because more buildings were constructed with brick and the hydraulic capabilities of the city had been improved somewhat. Most fire damage was thus limited to a couple of houses. But some outbreaks were considerable in extent. "Les heures perdues" records over thirty fires in the city. In 1748 the old opera house burned to the ground; and in 1772 the accidental igniting of some powder stored in the Hôtel de Ville caused 200,000 livres in damage.[27] A small house fire in 1779 burned out of control, destroying three buildings, because the water pumps failed to work.[28]

But these accidents were minor compared to the damage and hardship wrought by nature. Eighteenth-century Toulousains were hardly spared the ravages of weather. Periodic cold snaps caused widespread suffering among a populace normally accustomed to the mild climate of the Midi. Barthès records eleven winters when the cold reached threatening levels, freezing the Garonne and provoking general alarm. The poor and homeless were naturally the most vulnerable to the temperature's sudden plunge; many froze to death in the streets despite the authorities' laudable though feeble attempts to provide warmth by lighting fires in public spaces. But privation was general in such instances, for with the freezing of the Garonne the city experienced an energy crisis: its mills were rendered inoperative and wood, virtually the sole source of heat, could no longer be transported by barge. On at least two occasions the dearth of wood caused rioting; and, as they

[25] 701:1.   [26] 703:162.

[27] 699:283; 704:193–94.   [28] 705:181.

did in times of grain shortages, the capitouls were forced to control the sale of wood and order emergency provisioning. Many artisans resorted to burning their furniture in lieu of firewood.[29] During several springs, late cold spells destroyed budding vines and damaged recently planted crops, thus threatening both the city's food supply and the revenue of its many landowning inhabitants. The urban populace's vital link to the countryside, as both consumers and landowners, made the weather as urgent a concern for them as it was for peasants. When drought persisted, as it did in eleven of the forty-two years covered by Barthès's diary, they joined with the clergy in solemn prayers and public processions to beseech God for relief. Even excessive heat could exact a toll. Barthès recounts the astonishing fact that among the throngs who gathered to witness the staging of military maneuvers on an unseasonably hot day in April 1748, nearly three thousand were struck down by heat sickness and three hundred died.[30]

More than anything else, it was flooding that threatened the city and periodically wreaked havoc, in terms of both buildings and structures destroyed and lives lost. The Garonne was Toulouse's lifeline and raison d'être, but the city was at the mercy of its swelling waters as well. Barthès records significant flooding on twenty occasions—nearly half the years he kept his diary—mostly in the late spring and early summer when the rains come to Languedoc. The mostly lower-class inhabitants of the Island of Tounis, a parcel of land in the Garonne, were forced to flee with alarming regularity; by the end of the century the island had virtually been washed away by repeated flooding. Nuns and monks domiciled along the river's banks were also periodically turned into refugees by the swelling waters. In several years the rising tide washed over the city's bridges. In 1743 the rain continued for two weeks, causing the Garonne to swell, crest, and overflow

[29] 702:2, 706:30.   [30] 699:272.

for three days.[31] Barthès described the flooding in June 1765, which ruined mills and damaged several convents and bridges, as the worst since 1727.[32] Five years later much of the city was submerged and scores perished.[33] The next year the waters did not recede for eight days.[34] The following year the heavens again unleashed their torrents—to punish Toulousains for their depravity, commented Barthès. The suburbs were ravaged, and Tounis just about entirely destroyed. Sixteen people were lost. The damages were assessed at 790,990 livres.[35] As if the flooding that year were not enough, a month later, in July 1772, a sudden storm sending egg-size hailstones down upon the region ruined crops and shattered 40,000 livres' worth of windows in the city.[36]

Although by the latter part of the eighteenth century the plague was only a distant memory for Toulousains, the city was not exempt from epidemic sickness. In 1743 a "grippe" that affected head and kidneys struck the populace, killing, according to Barthès, over fifteen hundred people during Lent alone.[37] Three years later "an infinity of young children and other people of every station" were swept away by an illness our diarist identifies only as "the picote"; this seems to have been smallpox.[38] The most severe epidemiological crisis of the last decades of the Old Regime spared humans only to ravage the region's cattle—the great animal distemper epidemic of 1774–1775. Toulouse was deeply affected by this outbreak, not only because its food supply and livelihood were intimately linked to the countryside's well-being, but also because as a major agricultural entrepôt it had to submit to the draconian

[31] 699:118–19. [32] 703:189–91. [33] 704:123–25.
[34] 704:155–57. [35] 704:188–92. [36] 704:182–83.
[37] 699:116.
[38] 699:129. For the identification of "picote" (or "picotte") as smallpox, see D. Roche, ed., *Journal of My Life by Jacques-Louis Ménétra*, trans. A. Goldhammer (New York, 1986), p. 66n.78. The word, however, is not listed in the *Dictionnaire Occitan-Français*, ed. Louis Alibert (Toulouse, 1966).

quarantine measures instituted to contain the epidemic. Reading Barthès, one apprehends a populace gripped by crisis during the long epidemic: not only did royal troops occupy the city, but the clergy led expiatory processions and special prayers, including the Orison of Forty Hours. And the Holy Sacrament was exposed on the altars of all the city's churches as an additional supplicatory measure.[39]

These mishaps and disasters punctuate Barthès's diary with depresssing regularity, providing the backdrop for his mounting woe. His commentary, in the sense that it accents the suffering and misfortunes of his times, is not unlike that of another urban observer, a Lille artisan, whose diary has been summarized by Alain Lottin in these terms:

> The place accorded by Chavette in his book to catastrophes, subsistence crises, falling salaries and declining employment, bad weather, epidemics, confirms for us that he lived, along with his contemporaries, in close dependence on natural conditions, not only physically, but psychologically.[40]

The difference, however, is that Chavette was a contemporary of Louis XIV. Nearly a hundred years later, Barthès's diary demonstrates that, for ordinary people at least, more stayed the same than changed in the Old Regime.

Or did it? For, as we have noted, Barthès was pathologically prone to emphasize the worst in all matters, rendering a portrait of his society as depraved and doomed, his times as lurching from crisis to crisis. Social and economic historians, including those of Toulouse, have given us a somewhat different view of the eighteenth century, one that, if not grounds for an optimistic assessment of the late Old Regime, at least ac-

[39] 705:38–40, 84–85.
[40] Alain Lottin, *Chavette, ouvrier lillois: un contemporain de Louis XIV* (Paris, 1979), p. 155.

knowledges a growing prosperity, improved living conditions, and a general rise in civility. Not surprisingly, Barthès, this provincial reactionary, this bigoted Latinist, got things somewhat wrong. Perhaps one reason for this misreading of his times, apart from his gloomy temperament, is that he witnessed some genuinely disturbing events, especially to someone so fervently identified with the status quo and ruling hierarchy. In short, Barthès was watching his world fall apart.

The first blow was delivered in May 1762 when the campaign against the Society of Jesus commenced. Barthès does not rehearse the complex religious and political issues behind this prolonged campaign; nor does he discuss the machinations of the realm's parlements and how their Gallicanism managed to win over both public opinion and the monarch in securing the Jesuits' expulsion as an ultramontane, and thus foreign, threat to France. Perhaps he was ignorant of what was at stake. But his diary does document the process by which an institution that since 1564 had educated, confessed, counseled, and preached to generations of the faithful of Toulouse was uprooted from the city, its clerics hounded and persecuted.

It was in May and June 1762 that the parlement's *arrêt* against the Jesuits was published in the city. It ordered the Society to submit before the court its titles to its local properties as well as those relating to its establishment. Courses at the college were also suspended, the city's inhabitants banned from the Jesuits' premises. Soon after, another arrêt ordered the seizure of their properties. At this point Barthès does not seem to be convinced of the seriousness of the campaign, for he notes that the two arrêts were carried out "après plusieurs politesses."[41] In October, however, he announced "with profound distress the proscription of the Jesuits, their expulsion from their old domiciles." The event, which he predicted

[41] 703:88–89.

would be talked about in ages to come, moved him to mis-quote a couplet from Virgil as an aphoristic curse. In March 1763 the screw was turned tighter on the Jesuits: they were forbidden to wear their habits or to communicate with the Society's general or superiors, and they were ordered to leave their homes within fifteen days.[42] Other proscriptions and ha-rassments followed over the next months: the consignment of two pro-Jesuit tracts to the flames, the extraction from Society members of an oath to the king and the Gallican Church, the expulsion from the city of those former Jesuits who had not received permission from the parlement to remain, the sale of the Society's property, the destruction of its Maison Professe, and the exhumation of the Fathers' relics. This last humilia-tion evoked from Barthès the commentary that these holy re-mains would one day, "the day of vengeance, rise up against the cupidity of those who have had the temerity to violate the sanctuary of their repose."[43] A final "thunderbolt" came in August 1767 when the Jesuits were deprived of their pen-sions.[44] Barthès's chagrin at the expulsion of his cherished teachers was matched only by his incomprehension. When he learned that a butcher shop would stand on the spot of the razed Maison Professe, his consternation turned to horror. Observing the hounding of this religious order through Bar-thès's eyes—a nasty, uncompromising, often physical affair—one realizes that the Revolution's persecution of the ecclesias-tical establishment some thirty years later was not without a precedent in living memory.

The campaign against the Jesuits troubled Barthès's faith in the established order more than any other public imbroglio of his time. Another conflict, however, followed swiftly on its heels. In 1763 the Parlement of Toulouse, along with several other royal courts of the realm, registered its objection to a

---

[42] 703:125.　　　[43] 704:22.　　　[44] 704:49–50, 56.

new tax, actually a tripling of the vingtième, an assessment on revenue from land. This objection was tantamount to authorizing a tax strike, and the crown reacted accordingly. Royal troops led by the duc de Fitzjames, the king's commander in the province of Languedoc, moved into and occupied Toulouse. The duke ordered the house arrest of the magistrates of the parlement and had his troops seize their palace. A curfew was imposed, so concerned was he that the parlement's actions would inspire a popular uprising in support of the court's protest. Although released after the tax edict was modified, the magistrates were hardly mollified: they ordered Fitzjames's arrest for lèse-majesté, causing him to flee the province. The crisis dragged on for over three months, with local authority, embodied by the parlementaires, and royal power, personified by Fitzjames, at loggerheads in the most public and contentious manner. For Pierre Barthès, a good Frenchman loyal to both king and parlement, it was an episode that, like the campaign against the Jesuits, tore his world in half.[45]

This wrenching experience would be repeated in the third crisis. The magistrates of the parlement were again at the center of the conflict, but this time the very existence of their court was at issue. In 1771, the royal minister Maupeou succeeded in promulgating the most radical reform to date under the Old Regime: the elimination of the realm's parlements and their replacement with a different system of smaller courts staffed by royal appointees, whose positions were nonvenal and nonhereditary. For a city such as Toulouse, whose prominence since the mid-fifteenth century rested on its position as the seat of the region's preeminent court—and whose populace greatly depended upon the activities and expenditures of the Robe gentlemen—the Maupeou reforms were a traumatic blow indeed. Some of the magistrates of the old court ac-

[45] 703:140–49.

cepted positions on the new one; the rest were rudely exiled from the city by lettres de cachet. Barthès's commentary was terse: "I leave to those more learned than I to justify, as they wish, the present epoch."[46] The new judicial regime lasted as long as the reign under which it was promulgated. With the ascension of Louis XVI there was a return to the status quo ante. In 1774 the Parlement of Toulouse retook possession of its judicial seat to the populace's—and Barthès's— jubilation.[47]

Two points are worth mentioning about these three great crises that punctuate Barthès's diary. First is their provenance: they were all national in scope; indeed, they emanated from decisions made in Paris or Versailles. Of course, one cannot pretend that before the eighteenth century Toulouse or other provincial cities were immune from political, religious, or fiscal forces that descended upon the city from without. French and Toulousain history teaches otherwise. And yet there is something striking in the fact that the most disruptive events in the city's public life in the second half of the eighteenth century were essentially national episodes played out on the local stage—a fact that finds a parallel in the precisely contemporaneous, virtually unprecedented presence of royal troops in the city. The point is even more noteworthy when considered in the context of an increasing royal influence over local festive life, something we shall observe in a later chapter.

The second point is in the form of a question. One might legitimately ask why, if these internecine conflicts within the Old Regime establishment so traumatized Barthès, he did not give vent to his opinions in the pages of a diary that was, after all, essentially a private document. Others among his contemporaries were not so reticent. But Barthès seems to have been gripped by a sort of internal censor, a mechanism that for

---

[46] 704:150, 164–67.   [47] 705:47–59.

someone so emotionally invested in the ruling hierarchy was perhaps a more powerful inhibitor than formal censorship. Recent scholarship has emphasized the freewheeling, savage, even pornographic criticism that emerged from the pens of assorted journalists, publicists, philosophes, and other disgruntled writers in the late eighteenth century. Prerevolutionary France, despite the well-known travails of such philosophes as Voltaire and Diderot, now appears to have been a rather permissive era for those writers willing to put up with anonymity, clandestinity, and the somewhat marginal world of Grub Street.[48] Clearly, Barthès was not of this world, just as he was not the sort of person who would make vituperative, scatological attacks on the royal family and the like. And it is well to recall that most literate observers were like Barthès— either inhibited from expressing their critical views or so enthralled with the ruling hierarchy that criticism, even when warranted, did not come easily. One might conclude from this that Barthès's diary exhibits an act of transference: the projection of his profound disappointment with the conduct of the crown and other royal institutions onto his contemporaries—his neighbors and fellow Toulousains whose public behavior and morals he excoriated with mounting zeal.

DESPITE the progress made in the way of creating more open spaces in the city—esplanades, quays, promenades, plazas, and the like—most streets in eighteenth-century Toulouse remained as they had been for centuries—narrow, twisted, crowded, dark, and dirty. When a great personage made his ceremonial entry down these same streets, however, they

---

[48] Darnton, "The High Enlightenment and the Low Life of Literature," in *The Literary Underground of the Old Regime*, pp. 1–40; and Lynn Hunt, ed., *Eroticism and the Body Politic* (Baltimore and London, 1991), articles by Hunt and Sarah Maza.

would momentarily be transformed through the artifice of tapestry and statuary into a theater of homage. So too, on the occasions of religious pageants and civic festivals, the city's thoroughfares and plazas took on a solemn or festive look. Even on ordinary days unmarked by a grand fete or citywide celebration the streets were still the scene of one ceremonial display or another, usually a religious procession, for such public devotions were daily events. In short, the ceremonial city existed, not only sporadically, in the great festivals and pageants that punctuated the municipal calendar, but also in the daily rites and devotions that made up street life.

Although Barthès is a less than ideal observer when it comes to the profane and unofficial pastimes of the populace, preferring to dwell on those solemn and civic exercises that met with his approval, he does provide a glimpse now and again of popular life at street level. One disappointing lack in his diary is any description of carnival. He does mention it once, but only in the context of noting that the reception of a new *procureur général* was particularly festive because it coincided with the popular fete. Perhaps Barthès's Catholic sensibilities militated against acknowledging carnival as an integral part of the city's festive life, for by the mid-eighteenth century the church's disapproval of such profane celebrations had hardened into opposition. He is only a little less reticent about another well-known popular ritual, the charivari. Only one took place in Toulouse between 1738 and 1780, if Barthès's observations are to be trusted as complete. In April 1739 a rather noisy dispute between one Sieur Barrau and his wife provoked a charivari which attracted such a large crowd that the City Watch had to be called out. The crowd grew rowdy and the Watch ended up firing upon the revelers, wounding nearly a dozen.[49]

[49] 699:39–40.

The youths who presumably animated this charivari participated in another local popular rite about which Barthès is
more forthcoming. The *acampa* was an age-old Toulouse tradition in which gangs of youths, recruited from all classes,
armed with slingshots and other rustic weapons, would engage
in pitched battles lasting the better part of a day. The ritualized combat usually took place on Rogations Day, a time
when Christians traditionally participated in processions to
mark the bounds of their parishes. The acampa too was about
boundaries, for according to Catel and other local antiquaries,
the origin of the ritual combat dates to a period when the city
was divided into two sections, the Bourg and the Cité—a division that, according to one local historian, also corresponded
to warring parties during the Albigensian Crusade.[50] Thus, the
two youthful gangs would shout, "Down with the Bourg!" or
"Down with the Cité!" as they fought—perhaps thereby commemorating the most traumatic moment in the city's history.
Barthès dutifully, though disapprovingly, mentions its occurrence nearly every year in his diary, wearily noting the authorities' impotence in suppressing the violent encounter. To be
sure, the ritual could prove deadly: in 1741, a young combat-
ant, a tailor's son, was killed in the clash.[51] The next year the
two gangs joined to ransack the lodgings of the city's official
executioner who, along with his valet, had tried to break up
the melee.[52]

Other street activities were not so violent. Like his neighbors, Barthès enjoyed the periodic visits of various peddlers
and conjurers who regaled the populace with dramatic demonstrations of their cures. In 1737, an Italian "operateur"

[50] Catel, *Mémoires de l'histoire du Languedoc*, pp. 137–38; C. Barrière-
Flavy, "Un sport dangereux à Toulouse au XVIIIe siècle," *Revue historique
de Toulouse* 12 (1925): 188–92; "Toulouse jadis," *Revue des Pyrénées* 2 (1890):
847–48.

[51] 699:85.

[52] 699:194.

named Blaches hawked his all-purpose remedy in an outdoor theater he and his accomplices constructed in the Place du Salin. To prove the antidotal properties of his "orvietan," he had his Swiss servant swallow fifty-seven grams of arsenic followed by fourteen or fifteen, presumably dead, spiders. He survived. Afterward, Blaches and his troupe presented an outdoor circus, including a high-wire act performed by a sixty-seven-year-old woman.[53] Apparently the people expected their street healers to be street performers as well. In June 1746 another circus troupe took the stage in the Place du Salin. Led by one Mafioli, "Count-Paladin and First Surgeon to the Queen of Spain," their spectacle climaxed with an acrobat walking a tightrope while juggling four large balls. Barthès was impressed. Mafioli's troupe stayed in the city over a month.[54] The next appearance of street performers noted by Barthès was in 1754, when Jean Creci, another "operateur italien," rode into town, preceded by ten servants on horseback, to a fanfare of trumpets and drums. Creci himself was dressed in a gold and silver costume covered with brilliant gems. Like other conjurers, he offered a theatrical spectacle to the people who gathered in the Place du Salin, but also dispensed to sufferers his curative potion mixed, our disgusted diarist noted, with urine.[55]

All of the street performers mentioned in "Les heures perdues" hailed from beyond Toulouse. Many were foreigners, or at least passed themselves off as "Italians" or such, a sure means of attracting a crowd in search of the exotic. Street culture might have been popular, but it was not humdrum and not always homegrown. The people had a taste for things bizarre and foreign; and their taste was fed by a stream of performers and conjurers drawn to the big metropolis, where opportunities for appreciative audiences abounded. Like the emerging consumer economy, popular culture in the eigh-

[53] 699:1–2.   [54] 699:211–12, 218.   [55] 702:12–13.

teenth century was increasingly enlarged and stimulated by new influences and commodities. But what was new and appealing was also sometimes merely ludicrous. And some of the hucksters themselves were bizarre as well. In 1759, for example, the young male companion of an Italian hawker of potions named Tonini was treated by surgeons for a pulmonary malady. The examination revealed, however, that the youth, who had long shared Tonini's bed, was in fact a woman—a state of affairs about which Tonini swore complete ignorance. Under pressure from the authorities, the two were married immediately.[56] In the summer of 1769, a "beast"—really nothing more than some kind of bovine—measuring nine feet high and thirteen feet long was displayed to the curious. It was supposedly on its way to Paris to be presented to the king.[57] Ten years earlier a huckster had arrived in town to display a "savage" named Rogo, discovered, he claimed, by a Dutchman on the island of Cop. Rogo had a special gastronomic talent. Before a crowd he consumed the following items, meticulously inventoried by Barthès: four plates of stones, as large as nuts; two hand-sized pieces of marble; and some ordinary rocks. The meal, weighing twenty-four pounds altogether, was then washed down with a bottle each of eau de vie and wine, "drunk very quickly."[58] Barthès called the impresario a "charlatan." But the capitouls had auditioned his act and approved its continued performance in the city (although a long run is hard to imagine). Other hucksters were not so fortunate. In 1779, another "Dutchman," who claimed to have been the keeper of animals at Versailles, displayed a zebra to curious crowds in the Place Royale. Not only did it turn out that he held no such position at the royal court, but his zebra turned out to be a painted ass. The Dutchman was fined and banished from the city for fraud.[59]

[56] 702:175.
[58] 702:177–78.

[57] 704:110–11.
[59] 705:183–84.

As these examples indicate, the authorities attempted to monitor street life, or at least tried to ensure that the people were not exploited by outright frauds and con men. It was common for the authorities to take an interest in popular pastimes, if only out of concern for the preservation of public order. In some cases, of course, "popular" festivities were sponsored or encouraged by the officialdom. A good case in point is the "Fête des Rois." Each January 6, the festival of Epiphany, the bakers of the city ceremonially distributed cakes, commonly known as the "kings' cakes," to the populace, a tradition commemorating the gifts of the Magi. By the eighteenth century, however, it seems that the bakers were, more often than not, reluctant to fulfill their annual ritual obligation. As Barthès notes, many years they pleaded hardship and the excessive price of flour or eggs as a pretext for canceling the ceremony. Sometimes the capitouls heeded their plaint and authorized the fete's suppression. On other occasions, the capitouls had to threaten the bakers with a one-hundred-livre fine to force them to distribute the cakes. At least once, in 1760, the dispute escalated into judicial proceedings before the parlement in which the magistrates sided with the municipal authorities, joining them in insisting that the bakers perform as expected.[60]

Much that might appear as "popular" in the ceremonial city often entailed the authorities' support and direction or depended upon institutions that were only marginally popular in nature. The best example of the overlap of institutional and popular traditions is to be found in the ritual existence of the Basoche, the confraternity of clerks who served the courts of law. There were two companies of the Toulouse Basoche, one for the parlement, the other for the sénéchal, the latter tracing its existence to the early fifteenth century. By the eighteenth century, the Basoche seems to have had an ephemeral exis-

[60] 703:1.

tence, mobilized, with the permission of their respective courts, only on great festive occasions. Thus, Barthès notes, its last appearance was during the celebrations for the birth of the dauphin in 1729. The next was in 1762, to help celebrate the appointment of a new first president of the parlement. In December of that year the newly elected "king" of the Basoche and his entourage of festively uniformed courtiers paraded through the city, proclaiming with the parlement's permission their "authority." Now that its existence had been formally authorized, at least for a period, the Basoche could play a role in enlivening popular celebrations. For the Fête des Rois, for example, the young clerks again processed on horseback through the city, paying a visit to the parlement, which received them with all due honors. Barthès commented favorably on this "wonderful display of youth," this "ravishing spectacle that we are not accustomed to see."[61] But later that month, when the former king of the Basoche died, his commentary was less charitable. The entire confraternity attended the funeral in costume, drawing this sneering remark: "Whether this was the most frivolous and useless of honors I will let my readers decide, supposing that these memoirs have any. I will restrict myself to saying 'Vanitas, vanitatum et omnia vanitas.'"[62] It is likely, however, that Barthès's disapproval echoed the attitude of the magistrates of the courts who, along with other *bien-pensant* people, saw in the Basoche a kind of countercultural manifestation of festive pageantry and pretend chivalry, which mocked the *gravitas* and sobriety of the judicial elite these lowly clerks served.[63]

[61] 703:120.

[62] 703:120–21.

[63] See the comments of David A. Bell on the Parisian Basoche: "Although the clerks imitated the noblesse de robe in their 'court,' in their dress and bearing they took more closely after the noblesse d'épée. In keeping with their legends of past military prowess, they insisted on wearing colorful clothing—particularly red stockings—and on carrying swords. On both

If the streets of Toulouse were often the scene of festive gatherings and ritual displays, they were also sometimes the stage for demonstrations of a more violent and contentious sort. Street life was normally turbulent, rude, and promiscuous in the eighteenth-century city. Increasingly it was subjected to a beefed-up policing apparatus, as we have noted. And for good reason: rioting and violent social conflict marked public life in eighteenth-century Toulouse more than at any other time in its history since the Wars of Religion two centuries earlier.

Barthès gives us an account of several of the most notable of these disturbances. Especially frequent were uprisings among the inmates of the city's three prisons (those of the parlement, sénéchal, and Hôtel de Ville) who, often with the connivance of corruptible guards, managed to break out with alarming regularity. There were at least six prison breaks during the forty years Barthès kept his diary, several posing a considerable threat to the city. An attempted jailbreak in 1758, during which the prisoners wrested rifles from the soldiers guarding them, ended in a pitched firefight with the Watch and the maréchaussée, leaving dead and wounded on both sides. When forty prisoners managed to escape from the parlement's jail in 1766, they were responsible for a local crime wave of several weeks' duration. Five years later the same prison proved incapable of restraining the scores of cold and hungry inmates awaiting sentencing and punishment. They busted out with ease and then fought off the Watch by hurling tiles from the prison roof.[64] Like the swarming presence of

---

counts they repeatedly defied the parlement, which, in *arrêt* after *arrêt*, banned both weaponry and any apparel besides modest black." David A. Bell, "Lawyers and Politics in Eighteenth-Century Paris" (Ph.D. diss., Princeton University, 1991), p. 74.

[64] 699:5, 210; 702:135–36; 704:24, 133, 162 for the six prison breaks. The frequency of prison breaks in eighteenth-century Toulouse lends credence

predatory vagabonds, the city's bulging population of restive prisoners was a source of fear and consternation for many Toulousains.

But in times of dearth and heightened social tensions some of these same Toulousains found themselves caught up in violent disturbances. Two melees illustrate the periodic breakdown of civic order in the eighteenth-century city. That of 1747 was a classic grain riot: flour in short supply, rumors of secret stockpiling of grain by "monopoleurs," the seizure of stores of flour by a mostly female crowd, the hasty assurances from nervous authorities that bread would be sold at a fair price, barricades in the streets—and fighting between hungry artisans and laborers and the city militia lasting several days. When calm was restored, the authorities responded with swift and severe justice that led several of the uprising's reputed leaders to the scaffold. The next month, royal troops entered Toulouse to insure the imposition of civil order. Barthès, reflecting the common view, condemned the rioters but reserved his greatest contempt for those "bloodsucking" monopolists whose conspiratorial deeds, he was convinced, lay at the root of the uprising.[65] The bloody disturbance of 1778, which he described as "the most disastrous event in the city's memory," had a different origin. A shortage of grain was not the issue. Rather, it began with the refusal of an artisan to submit to service in the city guard, prompting other conscripts to go on strike against this hated "corvée." An angry crowd gathered, only to be met with a parlementary decree forbidding any congregating in public places. The next day,

---

to the notion of Peter Linebaugh that the period was not only the era of Foucault's "Great Confinement," but also, owing to the popular propensity for resistance and escape from confinement, a time of "excarceration." Peter Linebaugh, *London Hanged: Crime and Civil Society in the Eighteenth Century* (Cambridge, 1992), p. 3 and chap. 10.

[65] 699:252–55. See also Schneider, *Public Life in Toulouse*, pp. 315–16.

the last of Pentecost, a crowd of strollers got mixed up with the City Watch; in the confusion and alarm the panicky militiamen charged the gathering. A massacre ensued, with the soldiers firing upon people as they fled for their lives down back streets and alleys. "A quantity of people were killed" in this "horrible butchery," which Barthès, not normally given to criticizing the authorities, likened to the "worst sort of despotism."[66]

Another disturbance, also something of a riot, deserves mention, if only because it adds to our appreciation of how the city's public life in the eighteenth century was increasingly buffeted by forces emanating from Paris. Thanks to the research of Arlette Farge and Jacques Revel, we now have a detailed historical anatomy of the strange panic that seized the Parisian populace in 1750 over the supposed kidnapping of children by the police.[67] Barthès's diary does not permit us to add anything to their description of this panic; it merely demonstrates that the episode had an echo in his provincial city far from Paris. He notes that on June 10th—a few weeks after the Parisian events—rumors were rife in Toulouse that children were being kidnapped from the streets, provoking a violent "émotion" among the people. Some were arrested. This is all that can be gleaned from "Les heures perdues" on the subject. From another source we learn that the rumor was embellished with the incredible tale that the children were needed to satisfy an aristocrat's proclivity for periodic bathing in blood.[68] Clearly, the rumor had made its own "tour de France" in the space of a month, for there is mention that the "news" had come by way of Lyons. Interesting in itself, what

---

[66] 705:158–62; Schneider, *Public Life in Toulouse*, p. 316.

[67] Arlette Farge and Jacques Revel, *Logiques de la foule: l'affaire des enlèvements d'enfants, Paris 1750* (Paris, 1988).

[68] Rosoi, *Annales de la ville de Toulouse*, vol. 4 (Supplement aux *Annales de la ville de Toulouse*), p. 114.

this suggests is that nearly forty years before the "Great Fear"—the panic that ran throughout the French countryside, provoking peasant uprisings against an aristocracy that was supposedly plotting to slaughter them—the byways of paranoid rumormongering were already established in provincial France.

BARTHÈS the moralist was also something of a phenomenologist—if such an anachronism could be applied to an eighteenth-century diarist. This is to say that his observations remained fixed on the surface events of city life, never indulging in those detailed, seemingly endless catalogs of urban institutions that proliferated in late Old Regime France. We cannot rely upon him for a complete portrait of the city. For this, one would do better to turn to Jean-Florent Baour's *Almanac historique de Toulouse*, published annually from the 1750s until the eve of the Revolution, a guide Barthès certainly was familiar with and probably owned. Instead, "Les heures perdues" offers us a series of observations and impressions of those "events worthy of being passed down to posterity." That these same events, or at least the anecdotal, moralizing way in which he presents them, would not jibe with most modern historians' notions of worthiness is only one indication of the intellectual distance between us and him. For Barthès, his city was not merely the background for the events he recounts; in a sense it *was* these events. Toulouse and its institutions came to life in the streets, in the public comings and goings he was able to observe. And how could it have been otherwise for such an individual? Barthès held no position in the municipal, royal, or ecclesiastical institutions that composed the city's hierarchy of officialdom; nor was he a frequenter of the salons, academies, or Freemason lodges that made up *le monde toulousain*. Not quite an outsider, he was still not a privileged member of the social or political elite, despite the services he rendered to the city as a Latinist. He remained on the sidelines of official life, and it was from this perspective that he observed his cherished city. In following his gaze, we shall start with what was apparently one of his favorite haunts: the scaffold.

CHAPTER 3

JUSTICE IN THE STREETS

The fifteenth of this month at four in the afternoon in the Place Saint-Georges was hanged a young man of twenty-five to twenty-six years, well-built, son of a tailor from Roussillon who was captured the sixth in his country for . . . firing on passersby and his neighbors with a rifle and pistol, which he did many times, and most notably recently for having killed a miller merely for the pleasure of committing murder. . . . This young man was so taken with the horror of his crime and was so self-possessed that at the moment of being pushed requested the executioner to wait a little: having been granted this request, he asked all the spectators to pray for him and he made such a moving exhortation on the sad state he was in that he brought those in attendance to tears. He died quite resigned, which was generally noted. His body after the execution was handed over to the doctors who had it brought to their school of medicine near the Gray Penitents. . . .

"Les heures perdues," March 1768 (704:101)

INTERSPERSED among Barthès's accounts of religious processions, devotional rites, fireworks, civic festivals, funerals, ceremonial entries, and other displays are his descriptions of executions and corporal punishments. His diary records well over five hundred occasions when justice was meted out to criminals in the streets of Toulouse between 1738 and 1780. Most of these were public hangings and other forms of execution. Indeed, what one reads in the pages of "Les heures perdues" reflects the rhythm of ceremonial life in the provincial capital, a rhythm that often oscillated between the festive and the macabre. Barthès himself was sensitive to this rhythm, commenting once on the strange juxtaposition of two scaffolds side by side in the Place Saint-Georges, one erected for the Blue Penitents' fireworks display to celebrate the ascension of Louis XVI, the other awaiting the hanging and breaking on the wheel of two thieves.[1] Catholic ritual, of course, was often concerned with death, evoking the nearness of death, the martyrdom of the saints, Jesus' sacrifice, and other reminders of human mortality. But such baroque ceremony, however morbid and compelling, could not rival actual rites of death for realism and drama. And these, as Barthès abundantly demonstrates, were performed before the people of Toulouse with astonishing regularity.[2]

We must be careful to note, however, the limitations of Barthès's accounts of criminal justice as a source for the wider subject of eighteenth-century criminality. First, it is clear that, despite the frequency of executions and public punishments

[1] 705:79
[2] J.-C. Perrot has noted that with the ban on interring the dead inside the city limits in the 1770s, "death stopped being culturally familiar to men of the eighteenth century." The implications of this banishment of the dead are interestingly treated by Perrot in his *Genèse d'une ville moderne: Caen au XVIIIe siècle* (Paris, 1975), pp. 565–67. However, it would seem that, contrary to his claims, the persistent, and perhaps also increased, staging of executions in cities such as Toulouse and Caen in the late eighteenth century preserved the urban populace's traditional familiarity with death.

in his diary, he failed to record all such events. In one rather busy week for the executioner, for example, he simply notes that hangings occurred at least daily, neglecting to provide further details on the victims' crimes or the precise number of executions. And although he claimed to ignore readers' objections to the diary's apparent preoccupation with executions, it is more than likely that he took such objections as a license to be less than comprehensive in his account. Second, the number of executions held in Toulouse is by no means a measure of crimes committed in the city. The Parlement of Toulouse automatically reviewed all capital sentences for crimes committed in its *ressort*, a region extending from Guyenne and Gascony in the west to upper and lower Languedoc stretching eastward. And many, if not most, of those convicted criminals whose sentences the magistrates upheld were executed in Toulouse. In fact, the procedure usually called for the sentence to be carried out within hours of its confirmation. Thus, although the people of Toulouse were treated to a steady diet of executions, its source was not primarily local.

ONLY A small portion of Barthès's entries concern corporal punishments as opposed to executions. The fact that there was no compunction warranting the parlement's review of non-capital crimes probably explains why there were comparatively few public punishments, for most criminals convicted of these offenses were punished elsewhere in the ressort. Thus it is also likely that those criminals publicly punished were from the city. Most were thieves, and their punishments entailed branding, whipping, or display in the pillory and then confinement in the galleys, prison, or hospital, or banishment from the city. A few criminals suffered their public ordeal and then were released. Most punishments combined whipping with branding. Often a criminal was forced in addition to make an *amende honorable*—to kneel and beg pardon for his crime—especially if it involved an offense against a local institution or personage. For example, in April 1739 a thief was whipped, marked with a red-hot iron, and then marched to Saint-Nicolas to beg pardon for having stolen some objects from that church.[3] Two years later an apprentice miller, convicted of stealing grain, was whipped, taken to the cathedral to perform the amende honorable, and then escorted by a detail of fifty soldiers to the mills where he worked, and branded with the letters *GAL,* signifying the galleys to which he was condemned for ten years.[4] Thieves not bound to the galleys were marked with a *V* for *voleur.* In 1749 one convicted murderer and thief, somehow spared from the scaffold, suffered an especially brutal branding at the hands of the zealous executioner, who bore down so hard on his flesh that it was scored to the bone.[5] Several years earlier another victim of branding boasted of a novel, if odoriferous, remedy to efface the mark— the application of a herring compress to the burn.[6]

Even more than executions, which always involved more ceremony than the simple dispatching of the victim, public punishments could be prolonged and dramatized in order to convey a particular message to the populace. This was especially important in times of heightened social conflict. After the riots of 1747, the nervous authorities were intent on demonstrating their resolve in the face of contentious restiveness. In November of that year a master baker, guilty merely of verbally insulting the capitouls, was led, chained and manacled, through the streets to the Hôtel de Ville to beg pardon. All of his confreres were obliged to witness the spectacle. In addition, he was fined 133 livres and banished from the city for three years.[7] The presumed leaders of the riots underwent preliminary humiliations before their punishments. On successive days in January 1748, four of them, two men and two women, were escorted across the city by royal troops and the maréchaussée. If the purpose in this exemplary display was to

---

[3] 699:39.   [4] 699:36.   [5] 699:299.
[6] 699:146–47.   [7] 699:251.

impress the populace with justice's rigor and the city's newly acquired armed might, it also evoked their pity, for Barthès notes that the victims' misfortune "brought tears to everyone's eyes."[8]

Crimes of a sexual nature also received special treatment. Women caught sleeping with the royal soldiers billeted in the city met a painful and humiliating end. In February 1748, one such unfortunate, a mere adolescent, was punished in the Place Royale. Stripped to her underclothes, she was forced to distribute birch rods to the waiting soldiers arranged in corridor formation, then flailed as she walked between them.[9] A year later another woman, guilty of the same "crime," suffered a similar fate. Afterward she was led, "completely naked," notes Barthès, to the prison of the Hôtel de Ville.[10] Whether the implicated soldiers suffered any punishment is not revealed by our diarist.

But pimps were subjected to a quite rigorous regime of shaming and punishment. In June 1749, after a fifteen-year hiatus, the infamous "cage" was again put into service to punish a pimp from Toulouse. Forced to make an amende honorable at the cathedral, he was led, nearly naked, through the streets, coiffed with flowers and feathers, and yoked with a sign reading "Public Pimp." Over ten thousand people lined the banks of the Garonne to witness the public dunking. The crowd had to wait three hours for the spectacle to commence, for the executioner, a novice at this particular punishment, had considerable difficulty getting the cage to function. When he finally did, he performed his task zealously, for the pimp died four days later.[11] The standard shaming technique for pimps borrowed from the popular tradition of charivari: hence the helmet of feathers and flowers they were forced to don. Hence also the use of an ass to carry them through the streets.

---

[8] 699:257–59.   [9] 699:268–69.
[10] 699:305.   [11] 609:305–6.

In September 1769, a husband-and-wife team of pimps from Carcassonne was punished in the traditional manner. Each sported flowers and feathers, and each was yoked with a noose. The woman rode astride backward on an ass, while her husband followed on foot. The couple was taken to Carcassonne to suffer the same humiliation and then confined in the local hospital for life.[12]

In the 1760s, it appears as though the nature of public punishment changed somewhat in Toulouse. Heretofore, as noted, the prescribed ordeal involved whipping, branding, or both. In 1760 the practice of displaying criminals in pillories becomes common. Criminals were still whipped and marked: in December 1760, a man who stole a couple of fish suffered the usual battery of whip and hot iron, but not before he was exposed in the pillory for two hours on three successive days.[13] As with other thieves punished in this manner, the pillory was set up in the marketplace where the crime had been committed, a sign suspended above indicating the nature of the misdeed. In 1772, Barthès noted that, "conforming to the new jurisprudence in Paris," all criminals condemned to the galleys were to be exposed in irons during three consecutive markets.[14] The punishments described in the last decades of his diary, when exposure was the rule for noncapital crimes, bear out this prescribed change. The theft of bodies from the cemetery apparently warranted a more prolonged exposure. In July 1774, a body snatcher from Castres was locked in irons and exposed for several hours over a four-day period, during which he verbally insulted those who came to witness his ordeal.[15] Convicted whores also suffered a novel form of humiliation. Barthès notes in 1763 the first use of what he describes as "a sort of sawhorse" (*chevalet*), which a woman was forced to mount in the Place Royale.[16]

---

[12] 703:26–27; other examples, 703:139, 704:204. [13] 703:29.
[14] 704:175. [15] 705:24. [16] 703:148.

Shame and humiliation, in addition to the obvious pain inflicted upon such minor felons as petty thieves and prostitutes, were clearly an important component of public punishment. But the ritual of shame partook of the same ceremonial as rituals of honor. Like the religious ceremonies we will examine in the next chapter, most public punishments entailed a procession of sorts—an exercise in shaming in which the criminal was led through the streets, sometimes forced to make an amende honorable in a certain spot, sometimes whipped as he proceeded on his forced march. If nothing else, this reminds us that the procession was indeed the central feature of traditional Old Regime ceremony, both sacred and profane. It also points to the centrality of the body, both real and symbolic, as the centerpiece of much processional ritual. Religious processions bore a range of bodies: statues of saints, holy relics, icons of the Virgin, the Host itself. So too did the forced marches of convicted criminals, who, like Christ in the Passion, were often whipped as they stumbled down the city's thoroughfares.

But if Barthès's observations are to be trusted, around 1760 public punishment undergoes a transformation. The procession ceases to be a central feature of its ceremonial. Rather, convicted thieves and other felons still had to submit to a shaming ordeal, but one that had them exposed in a central spot, usually a marketplace or the Place Royale. A minor detail in itself, this change will take on added significance when we examine the larger arena of ceremonial life in the eighteenth-century city. For one significant feature was the new preference for stationary festivities as opposed to those, most notably the procession, that took the entire city as their stage.

DID Barthès have a taste for executions? If he did, he had plenty of occasions to satisfy it. Three hundred and thirty-one people were put to death in Toulouse between 1738 and

1780.[17] The capital of the region, Toulouse was also its hecatomb of criminal justice. In few other places in France, indeed in Europe, were people offered such a continuous spectacle of death and suffering. This point needs amplification, for a reader might be excused for concluding that the number of executions in eighteenth-century Toulouse was really not so large. Simple arithmetical division "proves," for example, that the average amounted to a mere 7.6 victims per year. The accompanying graph, however, demonstrates that in many years the figure was much greater, as high as twenty. There were, moreover, periods when the parlement sped up the judicial process in an attempt to empty the city's teeming prisons, the result being multiple executions in the course of a week or even a single day. The graph also shows that royal justice grew more severe between 1738 and 1780, with executions steadily increasing. This finding, which is in keeping with our general view of eighteenth-century justice's growing reliance on the scaffold, is underscored by the fact that as the period progressed, an increasing share of convicted felons died on the wheel—a painful and shameful ordeal. Finally, a look at the number of executions in other eighteenth-century cities confirms that Toulouse ranked among those venues where the spectacle of public death was most frequent (see table 2).

Most criminals met their death by hanging, but others were strangled first. Many were broken on the wheel, their four limbs smashed as they lay face heavenward, extremities ex-

---

[17] Although Barthès's count of the number of executions was not official, one can be reasonably certain of its rough accuracy. There is a digest of the executions ordered by the parlement for the years 1750–1778; the total comes to 231. A very few of the condemned were executed elsewhere in the region, but the overwhelming majority mounted the scaffold in Toulouse. A comparison of this list with Barthès's diary for the twenty-eight years they overlap confirms his observations, in terms of both numbers and specific executions, to a remarkable degree. See Archives départementales, 51 B 25–27.

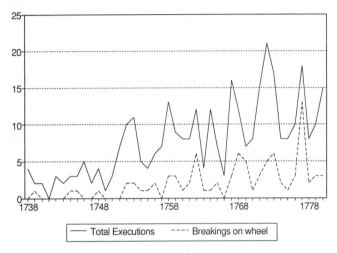

Executions in Toulouse, 1738–1780

tended. A few were burned at the stake. Some were mutilated or tortured before being dispatched by the executioner. Military deserters were executed by firing squad. Nearly every corpse was afterward left to rot either on the scaffold or on the *fourches patibulaires*, located just outside the city walls. It is safe to assume that on any given day eighteenth-century Toulousains were likely to have a body—in pain, dying, dead, or decaying—before their eyes.

On a few occasions the body itself, or a living one, was missing from the ritual of execution. Printed pamphlets and books judged either politically or religiously scandalous received the same treatment as convicted blasphemers. In 1771, a book entitled *Observations sur les protestations des princes du sang* was lacerated and then burned in the courtyard of the parlementary palace.[18] In 1775 and 1776, two other writings, one attacking the first president of the parlement, the other

[18] 705:43.

TABLE 2
Comparative Figures on Executions in
Several Eighteenth-Century
European Cities and Regions

ENGLAND	
Western Circuit: 1770–1794	308
Norfolk Circuit: 1768–1794	206
GERMANY	
Würzburg: 1769–1783	18
Mecheln: 1700–1795	23
Nuremberg: 1701–1743	69
THE NETHERLANDS	
Amsterdam: 1651–1750	390
FRANCE	
Flanders: 1721–1790	309 (condemnations)
Toulouse: 1738–1780	331

SOURCES
England: Clive Emsley, *Crime and Society in England, 1750–1900* (London and New York, 1987), pp. 209–11.

Germany: Richard van Dulmen, *The Theatre of Horror: Crime and Punishment in Early Modern Germany*, trans. Elisabeth Neu (Cambridge, 1990), pp. 43, 83.

Amsterdam: Pieter Spierenburg, *The Spectacle of Suffering: Executions and the Evolution of Repression* (Cambridge, 1984), p. 213.

Flanders: Pierre Deyon, *Les temps des prisons* (Paris, 1975), p. 97.

Toulouse: "Les heures perdues de Pierre Barthès."

criticizing plans for reforming municipal government, were destroyed in the same fashion.[19] The fact that a convicted criminal had managed to escape beyond the reach of the law did not halt his ritual execution: the burning or hanging of effigies, with all the solemnity and formality of a real execution,

[19] 704:159–60; 705:93–94.

was still practiced in eighteenth-century Toulouse. Having fled corporal justice, a criminal could expect the seizure of his property, as well as the infamy that the ritual execution of an effigy broadcast. Once a master printer was hanged in effigy while the books he printed for Huguenots were put to the flames.[20] Finally, on at least two occasions, the bodies of suicides were tried and gruesomely "executed." The procedure, followed to the letter in both cases, was first for the cadaver to be eviscerated, then filled with quicklime. Next it was placed on trial, with lawyers arguing for and against its guilt for the crime of suicide. If found guilty, the body was then dragged face down through the streets, strung up by its feet for a time, and finally thrown outside the city walls to be eaten by the dogs. Barthès, for once, demonstrated an uncharacteristic capacity for revulsion following the desecration of a suicide's body in April 1768. "The horror of this execution turned the stomachs of many witnesses, causing them to look away in disgust and heartache," he wrote. Perhaps this revulsion began to affect the authorities, for in 1775 they used the pretext that devotional books had been found in the home of a recent suicide as evidence to find him innocent of the crime, thus sparing his corpse the prescribed punishment and mutilation.[21]

Barthès was at his most loquacious when it came to executions. Although he was sometimes on the defensive, as we have noted, for filling his diary with the macabre accounts, he was far from reticent. Indeed, his commentaries on the last agonies of criminals are often hate-filled. The breaking on the wheel and strangulation of a man who murdered his brother evoked this diatribe on the victim's native land, an area heavily populated with Protestants: "This country of Vivarais, fertile in parricides and monsters of all sorts . . . points all too well to a ferocious and barbarous people without Religion, or humanity, though neighbors of our province."[22] Presumably he was speaking for more than himself when he noted a general satisfaction at the hanging of an inveterate thief of Toulouse in 1766, whose end "pleased all good people, seeing their city purged of this troublesome vermin."[23] His hatred was compounded by lust for cruelty, a disposition that was sometimes disappointed even by the cruel standards of eighteenth-century justice. Barthès called a young man who had attempted to murder his father a "monster of nature," and expressed outrage that he was sentenced to the "light penalty" of hanging rather than a more prolonged and painful death.[24] Indeed, the epithet "monster of nature" flows readily from his pen to describe several victims of justice. He was, however, not without pity for some, especially if they were young, female, and pretty. The hanging in February 1767 of a "very pretty" girl of seventeen or eighteen, guilty of stealing a pittance from her master, caused "general complaining" at the severity of the punishment. But Barthès mused that "it is necessary for such examples in order to control domestics, who hold the lives and wealth of their masters in their hands."[25]

Most executions took place in the Place Saint-Georges, located in the parish of Saint-Etienne in the northern half of the city. Today the plaza is one of Toulouse's fashionable spots, a pleasant square bordered by expensive restaurants and tastefully restored Old Regime buildings. In the eighteenth century it was already the center of a prosperous quartier inhabited primarily by magistrates and other officers. As one of the city's larger plazas, it was frequently the site of fireworks and other festive displays, as well as hangings, breakings on the wheel, and the like.[26] The ritual of execution was not enacted in a marginal space (like London's Tyburn) but in a central

[23] 704:27. [24] 704:84. [25] 704:43.

[26] But not for markets, at least after 1779. In that year a proposed move of a market from the plaza in front of the Hôtel de Ville to the Place Saint-Georges was reconsidered precisely because of the frequency of executions there. The market was instead moved to the Place Daurade (705:179–80).

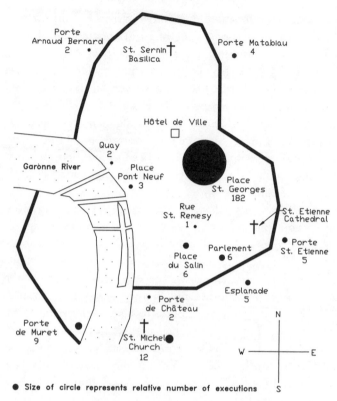

Places of Execution in Toulouse, 1738–1780

square accessible to Toulousains of all sorts.[27] Some executions were held elsewhere in the city. Before the eighteenth century, the Place du Salin, the square in front of the parlement's palace, had been a prime spot for executions. It was there that Lucilio Vanini, the infamous philosopher-magician, was burned at the stake in 1619. During Barthès's time, however, the plaza was only rarely the stage for the last episode in the

[27] It appears that in the first part of the nineteenth century, there was a trend in French cities to move the spot of execution from the center to the

criminal justice process. On occasion executions took place inside the courtyard of the parlementary palace, presumably when a more public display was deemed inadvisable. When the victims were prisoners guilty of rioting or trying to escape, however, the choice of the palace courtyard was not a matter of caution, but rather in the interest of setting an example. In August and September of 1758 two leaders of a prison revolt were hanged outside the windows of the parlement's prison, its inmates forced to witness the spectacle.[28] Deserters from the royal regiments also sometimes faced the firing squad there, although most were dispatched on the banks of the Garonne. Often criminals were hanged outside one of the city gates. Were these cases when the misdeed had been committed in a town or village located in the direction of the road leading from Toulouse, thus allowing the news of the criminal's shameful end to find its way back to the scene of the crime? Or did the court simply reserve some executions for the edification of the inhabitants of the faubourgs and the many voyagers entering the big city? It is difficult to say. Marketplaces were also sometimes the site of executions. And, as with corporal punishments, sometimes the scaffold was erected on the spot of the crime. In July 1776, for example, a female servant who had stolen eight hundred livres and some items from her mistress, a barrister's widow, was hanged on Rue Remesy in front of her employer's house. The narrow street could barely contain the "incredible crowd" that gathered, resulting in near suffocation of some of the spectators.[29]

As executions in eighteenth-century Toulouse—and in Amsterdam and Paris in approximately the same period—

---

urban periphery. In Paris, for example, the site was changed from the Hôtel de Ville square to the nearest city gate. The same shift can be observed in Bordeaux, Alençon, and Le Puy, among other cities. John Merriman, *The Margins of City Life* (New York and Oxford), pp. 18–19.

[28] 702:140–42.   [29] 699:214.

took place primarily in one central spot, they also tended to be staged at the same time of day. Late afternoon, not daybreak or the proverbial high noon, was the preferred moment for an execution. There were, however, curious exceptions to this rule. A highwayman was broken on the wheel and finally strangled at midnight in August 1771.[30] And in June 1767 a notorious thief named Laroche, who had also participated in a great prison break, had his rendezvous with the executioner at three in the morning.[31] But a late performance did not deter people from attending the theater of death: the execution of a whole gang of criminals—three men and two women— staged well after midnight drew over two thousand spectators in 1768.[32] So did another nocturnal breaking on the wheel in August 1771—although Barthès was forced to admit that people were enticed to come out as much by the pleasant summer night as by their concern to see justice done.[33]

The usual reason for these late executions was that preliminary proceedings could drag on for hours or even days. One potentially time-consuming aspect of the execution ritual was the last testament, delivered at the foot of the scaffold in the presence of a scribe and the capitouls. What interested the authorities in this procedure was the possibility that the certainty of near death, in concentrating the mind, might prompt the victim to incriminate others or name his accomplices. Often the testament worked to their satisfaction. A porter who was about to be hanged in September 1764 suddenly began naming "an infinity of people of each sex and every age," who were then brought to the scaffold to confront their accuser. Three of them were hanged later that month.[34] A man facing the gallows for attempted murder in 1758 was so long-winded in his accusatory testament that a chair and table had to be fetched to accommodate the exhausted scribe.[35]

[30] 704:160.   [31] 704:50–51.   [32] 704:84.
[33] 704:158.   [34] 703:169–70.   [35] 702:134.

When in 1765 a man of seventy slated to hang for cattle theft named a female inmate in the sénéchal prison as his main accomplice, he not only satisfied the authorities but also managed to delay his execution for a time.[36]

Another preliminary procedure that could postpone an execution was torture. It is not clear from Barthès's diary precisely how many criminals were tortured to secure additional evidence concerning either their own guilt or the guilt of others. Nor does it seem that the records of the parlement are a dependable source on the frequency of "the question ordinary and extraordinary."[37] But that torture was common is clear from the cases where Barthès does decide to note its application. He cites nineteen criminals who were subjected to "the question." Most of these were thieves, some guilty of both theft and murder. One was a counterfeiter, another the leader of a prison revolt. What seems to have been paramount in the judges' minds in deciding whether to apply torture was the likelihood of discovering accomplices. Common to most of the victims was thus the collective, or presumably collective, nature of their crimes. The precise nature of the torture could vary. Usually the "extraordinary question" mandated pumping water into the victim's mouth. In March 1778, a woman convicted of poisoning her husband was ordered to be put to the "question." Some confusion arose, however, for it had been forty-three years since a female had been subjected to judicial torture. A few days' research into the matter produced a suitable ordeal: basically a bone-crunching device applied to the victim's legs. Afterward, the woman was strangled and burned at the stake.[38] Abolished in the realm in 1780, the

---

[36] 703:193.

[37] In her study of eighteenth-century criminality in Languedoc, *Justice et répression en Languedoc à l'époque des lumières* (Paris, 1980), Nicole Castan does not discuss the issue.

[38] 705:148.

practice of judicial torture remained an instrument in the Toulouse magistrates' arsenal of criminal justice up until the hour of the reform.

Even without torture, the way to the scaffold and the criminal's final agony could prove prolonged and dramatic. On occasion, the drama was provided by the executioner himself. Spectators, including Barthès, were interested not only in how a criminal faced his death but also in how the executioner performed his task. Mishaps did occur, usually when the professional executioner was absent or indisposed, but even a seasoned professional could find dealing death hazardous. Once, in 1745, in the course of the breaking of a murderer's limbs, the wheel suddenly collapsed, sending both victim and executioner crashing to the pavement.[39] When, in September 1762, the executioner fell ill, his valet stepped into his shoes—with disastrous results. He botched the breaking on the wheel of a convicted murderer, smashing his head, thus incurring the fury of the crowd.[40] In July 1769 the pace of executions was so frantic that the executioner's son was put to the task. Then again a blow aimed at a victim's arms came crashing down on his head instead—for which maladroitness the young apprentice was put in prison.[41] At his debut in 1757, a novice executioner, hired to replace the old one sacked for drunkenness, proved unequal to the task. He nearly fell to his death when his foot caught in the ladder as he tried to hang a convicted thief.[42] It was no fault of the executioner's that the city did not possess a proper ax for the beheading of a nobleman guilty of kidnapping a young lady in July 1759. But, owing to this lack, the execution had to be delayed for several days while a blacksmith prepared an appropriate blade. Barthès notes that the blacksmith had to be provided with a detail of guards to prevent crowds from gathering to spur him on with his task—

[39] 699:185–86.
[41] 704:109–10.

[40] 703:108.
[42] 702:99.

so eager were they to witness the beheading, a method of execution not seen in Toulouse since 1678. Alas, the people were ultimately disappointed, for the delay had enabled the young nobleman's parents to secure a royal order overruling his execution.[43] However prolonged the drama of an execution's preliminaries, normally it terminated with the death of the criminal. Not so in March 1751, when a thirty-year-old highwayman from Montpellier was hanged. As was sometimes the case, the thief's body was handed over to the city surgeons for their anatomical lessons. The surgeons discovered that they had acquired, not a corpse, but a still warm body which, once bled, fully revived. Barthès does not tell us whether the young man survived only to face the hangman again.[44]

In his celebrated study *Discipline and Punish*, Michel Foucault suggested that executions were occasions allowing for the exercise of free speech, something otherwise largely forbidden in the public arena of the Old Regime.[45] In late-eighteenth-century Toulouse, however, few criminals took advantage of their last moments on the scaffold to speak their minds. Most died resigned to their fate, a few truly penitent. Some provided an edifying spectacle of the contrite Christian, prepared to face God's judgment. A criminal usually marched to the scaffold accompanied by a priest, who exhorted him to confess and offered consoling prayers. The spectacle of a boy of eighteen, about to be hanged and burned for poisoning a friend, limply passing from the arms of a priest into the executioner's embrace, touched the hearts of the assembled, reported Barthès.[46] Another even younger boy, a convicted thief, cried out

[43] 702:163–64.

[44] 700:17. For a similar case in eighteenth-century Paris, see Arlette Farge, *Fragile Lives: Violence, Power and Solidarity in Eighteenth-Century Paris* (Cambridge, Mass., 1993), p. 188.

[45] Michel Foucault, *Discipline and Punish: The Birth of the Prison*, trans. Alan Sheridan (New York, 1979), p. 60 and passim.

[46] 705:121.

before he was hanged that "he was going straight to heaven which he saw opening above him."[47] Many victims made a simple declaration of regret for their crimes before dying; and when they did, Barthès gave them credit for their contrition. For example, he declared "very edifying" the testimony of a young rapist who "displayed so much regret for having offended God and so much submission to his will."[48] In 1771, the executioner finally had to wrench the crucifix from the grasp of a convicted murderer, so intent was he on repenting for his crime.[49] While languishing broken on the wheel, one victim kept calling out "for mercy to the Lord."[50] Another "prayed to God until the last moment of his life."[51] Some were more long-winded and articulate, providing truly animated spectacles to the assembled. In 1764, an invalid guilty of stealing a couple of mules delivered a long confession to the crowd on his sinful ways and the evil company he kept.[52] Five years later, a convicted murderer actually halted the hangman in mid-execution, turned to the crowd, orated at length on his life of misdeeds, and supplicated them to pray for his miserable soul. His exhortation was so pathetic that it moved the people to tears.[53] Just before being hanged in 1772, a thief pleaded with the mothers and fathers assembled to watch carefully over their children.[54] In 1776, a young servant of a magistrate, guilty of murder, behaved "admirably and piously" as he mounted the scaffold to be broken on the wheel. He greeted the assembled, embraced and kissed the attending priests, and confessed to his crime. Tied to the wheel, he began to chant "songs in honor of the birth of the Lord" before submitting to the executioner's blows.[55] An enterprisingly

[47] 701:41. [48] 701:54. [49] 704:158.
[50] 703:70. [51] 704:2. [52] 703:166–67.
[53] 704:101. [54] 704:180.
[55] 705:107. Foucault wrote that "such speech is too close, even in its turn of phrase, to the morality traditionally to be found in the broadsheets and pamphlets for it not to be apocryphal" (*Discipline and Punish*, p. 66). The evidence assembled here would seem to argue otherwise.

pious approach was demonstrated by a laborer slated to be burned alive for the theft of sacred vases in May 1780: he had a friend print up and distribute leaflets calling upon people to pray for his soul.[56]

If some victims displayed such signs of contrition and piety, others simply went mad at the sight of the scaffold. One thief "lost complete control of his senses."[57] Another bellowed horribly as he lay broken on the wheel, shocking even the jaded spectators who had, after all, extensive exposure to public suffering.[58] A man slated to hang for shooting and wounding a servant during a drunken brawl refused to stand up in the chariot that transported him to the scaffold, remaining glued to the floor "like a frog."[59] Such examples could be multiplied. A man convicted of theft in September 1773 was surely not unique in slipping into a state of total catatonia at the reading of his sentence: the executioner had to carry him up onto the scaffold.[60] Extreme cases of madness warranted a delay in the execution. A female thief in her early twenties, "with a very pretty figure," Barthès informs us, would have been executed promptly after sentencing if she had not fallen into a delirium, thus giving her a reprieve of several days.[61] Another execution was postponed to allow the victim, a man from Montpellier sentenced to hang for murder, to revive from a two-week trance, during which time he took neither food nor liquid.[62] Feigning madness was just one strategy criminals tried in hopes of avoiding or postponing their fate: in November 1762 a man convicted of murder started to "play the imbecile" as soon as his sentence was read and continued acting the part, singing at the top of his lungs, all the way to the scaffold.[63] Another strategy was to make a declaration of pregnancy: between 1738 and 1780 at least five women awaiting the gallows claimed they were with child. One woman had the temerity

[56] 706:22. [57] 704:55. [58] 704:46.
[59] 704:3. [60] 705:5. [61] 703:22.
[62] 704:77–78. [63] 703:114.

to make the claim twice. Indeed, all were lying, but their ruse proved partially successful since each had to be examined by a doctor, thus delaying the execution for a couple of days.[64]

Criminals occasionally did live up to Foucault's image of the condemned man freely speaking his mind during his last moments alive, seizing the scaffold as a soapbox. Most simply—and vigorously—protested their innocence. Some contested the system of justice itself. One young man, convicted of murder, refused to listen to the confessor, who counseled him to forgive his enemies, declaring that it was his judges who were the guilty ones.[65] Victims were normally asked by the attending priest to pardon their judges, which occasionally elicted a predictably sour response. After scoffing at this suggestion, one man spat out to the executioner that he should "do his duty."[66] Another mocked the assembled officials and spectators, making light of the life he was about to lose.[67] Protestants were notably contentious victims, especially when it came to the clergy's exhortations. Like most of his coreligionists who found themselves on the scaffold in Toulouse, a Calvinist convicted of killing his father-in-law refused to accept the priest's pleas to repent, declaring that "it was not up to him to judge him." The priest proved less than charitable and responded that the condemned man was therefore "going to burn in hell that very evening."[68] Once a condemned Huguenot debated "shoulder to shoulder" with the priest who rode with him to the scaffold, finally forcing him off the chariot. He refused to make an amende honorable and even threatened the executioner.[69] Another Protestant, convicted of raping a young girl, provided an afternoon's entertainment for the crowd. First he haughtily refused to make an amende honorable, declaring loudly that the judges persecuted the inno-

---

[64] 702:1–2; 704:203; 705:125, 137, 146.   [65] 703:23.
[66] 704:187.   [67] 704:182.   [68] 701:57.
[69] 704:123.

cent while letting murderers and thieves run free. He angrily confronted the confessor, seized his snuffbox (!) from his hands, and threw it into the crowd. Then he suddenly turned compliant. Having initially refused to confess, he now declared that he had undergone a change of heart. Unbound, he was escorted to a notary's office where, his compliancy proving to be a ruse, he temporized for nearly two hours. He would satisfy neither the judges with a confession nor the confessor with a conversion. And so he found himself back on the scaffold, which he mounted while laughingly warning the hangman, "You'd better be careful." Turning next to the crowd he announced, "Messieurs, I am as innocent as a newborn baby." The executioner informed him that he would have to hang anyway. "Then let's go," he shouted, and jumped, without assistance, from the end of the rope.[70] The execution of a notorious Calvinist minister, whose father and grandfather had both died on the scaffold for their faith, apparently warranted extra security measures by the authorities. The Place du Salin was occupied by the royal regiments de Berry, and the minister's last words, really a sermon, were cut short by the troops' drumroll.[71] Later that same day, three Huguenot gentlemen who had tried to rescue him from prison were beheaded, their executions attracting an overflow crowd of spectators who hung from windows and stood on rooftops to catch a glimpse of the bloody scene. Again, armed royal troops guarded the spot.[72]

It was not really unusual to find royal troops or some other armed forces present at executions. When the suspected leaders of the 1747 riots were hanged, the Gantes Volontaires regiment, the maréchaussée, and the Watch combined in a show of force and surrounded the scaffold with fixed bayonets, some facing the scene of execution, others menacingly pointing

[70] 701:46.   [71] 703:67.   [72] 703:68–69.

their muskets at the crowd.[73] This was, to be sure, a highly charged situation, warranting an intimidating display of force majeure. But while the presence of royal troops at executions was relatively infrequent, the participation of forces other than the City Watch—who always marched the criminal to the scaffold—was not. The maréchaussée was almost always in attendance, supplementing the Watch with their mounted force. Perhaps this armed presence, comprising both traditional and extralocal forces, explains why executions in eighteenth-century Toulouse—unlike elsewhere, most notably Tyburn—never occasioned rioting or popular protest that Barthès deemed worthy of noting.

While most executions were by hanging or a combination of breaking on the wheel and strangulation (see table 3), some involved even more painful ordeals. At least six convicted criminals suffered the agony of having their right hands cut off. In two cases the crimes were heinous acts of patricide and infanticide: a son's killing of his father, and a man's hacking to death of his four children. But the other four cases, all thefts of sacred objects from churches, can hardly be deemed particularly monstrous crimes, even allowing for the heightened Catholic sensibilities of the Toulouse magistrates—those persecutors of Calas. These were, of course, crimes against God and religion, acts of desecration requiring not only punishment but also expiation. This was especially true in the case of two men who had stolen a vase containing the Host. In January 1771 these desecraters were first mutilated and then burned alive.[74]

Indeed, seventeen criminals were burned at the stake in Toulouse between 1738 and 1780. In addition to the two men just mentioned, two others were found guilty of stealing "sacred objects." One man was convicted of parricide and was

---

[73] 699:260.

[74] 704:148; for the other cases: 699:97; 701:37, 49; 703:100; 704:61, 158.

TABLE 3
Methods of Execution in Toulouse, 1738–1780

Hanging:	211	Burning alive:	14
Breaking on the wheel live:	57	Firing squad:	10
Breaking on the wheel with		Strangling, then burning:	3
preliminary strangulation:	30	Beheading:	3

burned only after being broken on the wheel (he may have already expired). The remaining six victims were all guilty of poisoning members of their families. One man disposed of his fiancée's three children in such a fashion. Two others were women, one convicted of poisoning both her mother and her husband. Barthès comments on the comportment of this "old" woman (she was forty) as she awaited the executioner's torch: "She looked with a cold eye on the instrument of her punishment, comfortably seated on the pile of faggots, a sight that made everyone shiver."[75]

Despite these gruesome cases of mutilation and burning, most criminals convicted of capital crimes died at the end of a rope. Two hundred and eleven of the executions in Toulouse, that is, about two-thirds of those noted in Barthès's diary, were by hanging. In some cases, the executioner strangled the victim as well. Breaking on the wheel was the next most favored method. There were in fact three ways in which criminals died on the wheel. Some were strangled immediately; most were left to languish for a period prescribed by the court—usually two or four hours—after which they were put out of their misery by strangulation; and a few were left to perish in agony without benefit of a coup de grace. One man took twenty-four hours to expire.[76] Jean Calas died on the

[75] 704:44–45; for other cases of burnings: 704:122, 148; 705:42, 146; 706:22.
[76] 702:48.

wheel but received the grace of strangulation after two hours of the ordeal, during which he persevered heroically.[77] The cases of execution by firing squad involved only soldiers. Then it was the custom for the victim's peers to take up a collection for his burial.

The ritual of execution did not end with a criminal's death. It continued with the deposition of his corpse. In a few cases, bodies were interred in a cemetery reserved for criminals outside the city. As the century advanced, an increasing number of corpses, especially females, were donated for dissection to either the city's corps of surgeons or those on the university's faculty of medicine. But most were left to rot, some in place, others on the fourches patibulaires. The fourches could accommodate a dozen or more bodies, and, given the pace of executions in Toulouse, it was often laden with corpses. Its purpose, of course, was to desecrate criminals' bodies, compounding the dishonor of the unburied with the humiliation of mutilation and dismemberment, for dogs often fed on the remains. On one occasion, however, the site turned into a place of honor. After the grain riots of 1747, the bodies of the executed leaders were displayed on the fourches. Crowds began congregating on the spot, and people claimed that the sky turned colors overhead. Some took bits of clothing and even pieces of skin from the bodies of the "martyrs." For once, the authorities decided that an early burial was in order.[78] In 1759 and again in 1777, the fourches were reconstructed, the second occasion in honor of the king's brother's visit to the city. The authorities were particularly anxious to alter the scaffold so that the corpses would hang above the reach of rav-

[77] 703:71; see also Bien, *The Calas Affair*, pp. 22–23.
[78] 699:265–67. It was thought by many that the remains of executed criminals possessed magical properties. In Paris in 1777, the charred bones of a criminal who had been burned at the stake were hawked to a crowd by day laborers; purchasers were convinced that the remains could insure luck in the lottery. Jeffrey Kaplow, *The Names of Kings* (New York, 1972), p. 138.

enous dogs—not out of concern for the criminals' remains but because parts of bodies kept showing up in dog owners' homes.[79] Barthès no doubt thought he was indulging in a bit of lighthearted gallows humor when he wrote that the exposure of a particularly fat man, a convicted thief, on the fourches would "provide the birds with food for many days."[80]

THAT public executions almost dominate the pages of "Les heures perdues" really proves nothing about ceremonial life in eighteenth-century Toulouse. It only demonstrates Barthès's taste for the macabre and for the suffering of others. If he had been less inclined to indulge this taste and more attentive to the routine, his entries would more faithfully reflect the daily processions and other public rites that far outnumbered these spectacles. Still, even if executions were not the most prevalent public ceremonies, their frequency cannot but astonish—a reminder not only of the severe nature of criminal justice in the eighteenth century but also of how the drama of life and death was so routinely enacted before people's eyes.

Personal taste aside, Barthès's satisfaction in witnessing a procession of criminals mount the scaffold reflected a no doubt typical, although somewhat extremely held, belief not only in the necessity of capital punishment as an instrument of justice but also in the salutary social effect of the repeated spectacle of execution. Viewed from the scaffold, the system of Old Regime justice looks cruel and vindictive indeed. But it is important to note that French jurisprudence mandated a whole series of legal safeguards against arbitrary punishment, and that the parlement, in particular, automatically reviewed all capital cases, thus acting as a buffer against possible irregularities in lower courts.[81] Of course this did not ensure that

[79] 702:172; 705:134–35.
[80] 706:25.
[81] See Bien, *The Calas Affair*, pp. 95–97. For the French parlements' role

justice would always prevail, especially in the case of Hugue-nots, as Jean Calas and others discovered. Nor did it mitigate the appalling severity with which many minor crimes, like simple theft, were treated. But just as the Revolution cannot be symbolically reduced to the guillotine (despite some histo-rians' claims), so Old Regime justice should not be equated with the scaffold, despite the fact that it tends to look that way through Barthès's vengeful eyes.

How then to think about these rites of death? They were indeed rituals, and thus we should place them in the context of the ceremonial city we are reconstructing on the basis of "Les heures perdues." In a sense, the death of the condemned was no different from that of any other Christian: a mystery worthy of the ritual attentions of the church. But as well, exe-cutions and corporal punishments, like most religious cere-mony of a public nature, partook of the processional form; criminals were routinely marched through the streets as a preliminary humiliation to their final ordeal.[82] On the scaf-fold religious devotions were paramount; clergymen offered prayers and exhorted victims to confess. Often they would re-spond with a truly Christian death. And sometimes the occa-sion was transformed into a moment of collective devotion, as the crowd fervently responded to the expiring person's prayers and pleas.[83]

---

in an earlier period as a check on the decisions of lower courts, see Alfred Soman, "Les procès de sorcellerie au Parlement de Paris (1565–1640)," *An-nales: ESC* 32 (1977): 790–814; and "La Décriminalisation de la sorcellerie en France," *Histoire, économie et société* 4 (1985): 179–203.

[82] In England, however, the procession ceased to play a role in the execu-tion ritual in the 1780s. Peter Linebaugh, "The Tyburn Riot against the Surgeons," in *Albion's Fatal Tree: Crime and Society in Eighteenth-Century England*, ed. Douglas Hay et al. (New York, 1975), p. 67.

[83] An eighteenth-century Caennais observer recorded an extraordinary case of the crowd and victim—a priest, lying broken on the wheel—chant-ing responsively a whole series of prayers. "After having finished the first

The political meaning of the execution was no less apparent, not only in the brute demonstration of deadly authority at the state's command, but perhaps more importantly in the crowd's ritual complicity in the act itself. Barthès can be read as a kind of spokesman for the people, some of whom, at least, must have shared in his approval of these rites to which they repeatedly returned. Even if their feelings were more mixed or somewhat sympathetic toward the victim—as was manifestly sometimes the case—the very structure of the execution created the conditions by which a certain public was convoked as participants and witnesses. The intent was "to make everyone aware, through the body of the criminal, of the unrestrained presence of the sovereign. . . . The justice of the king was shown to be an armed justice."[84] And usually this armed aspect of the judicial process was demonstrated not only on the condemned's body but also by the presence of royal troops. In lieu of an adequate policing apparatus, the crown relied upon the spectacle of the execution and the concomitant, concentrated display of force majeure to project its authority. Such, it is assumed by historians,[85] was the logic of criminal justice in the Old Regime; not quite the "policy of terror" that Foucault describes, it yet aimed to instruct and deter through repeated, terrible examples.

But the logic was rent by a contradiction, evident precisely

---

verse [of the 'Veni Creator'], the public sang the second; the victim took up the third, and thus it continued until the end. After which, the victim intoned and sang the 'Ave Maria' up until the end of the verse; the public sang the second, the victim the third, and thus to the end. He then told the executioner to pray ask the people to say a 'Miserere' for him in Latin, during which he would recite it in French." "Journal de Jacques Muger, avocat au Roy à l'Hôtel de Ville de Caen, 1758–1762," in *Recueil de Journaux Caennais, 1661–1777*, ed. G. Vanel (Paris and Rouen, 1904), pp. 174–75.

[84] Foucault, *Discipline and Punish*, pp. 49–50.

[85] See, for example, Cameron, *Crime and Repression*, pp. 10, 156; and Castan, *Justice et répression*, p. 286.

in the elevated number of executions staged in Toulouse. On the one hand, provincial capitals like Toulouse, sites of royal courts, served as privileged theaters for executions because at this level of the criminal justice system it was only the king—through his agents, the royal magistrates—who could inflict the greatest penalty. The logic of absolutism obliged the clustering of executions in these cities, but at the expense of the logic of deterence. For the latter would presumably have stipulated setting an example by staging frequent executions elsewhere in the region. The result was that the fifty thousand or so inhabitants of Toulouse, and its many visitors, had the privilege of witnessing an endless series of executions, while those who resided in the communities where the capital crime was committed were either denied the satisfaction of seeing justice done or spared the cautionary lesson enacted on the scaffold. No wonder privileged observers like Barthès became connoisseurs of the spectacle. But should not this contradiction in the system cast some doubt on the assumption that executions were largely conceived to compensate for an under-policed populace?[86] Might this assumption rather reflect a desire among modern historians to find a rationale for a system otherwise marked by indiscriminate cruelty and excess?

More than anyone else, Michel Foucault has tried to avoid viewing the execution in such functional terms, preferring to see it as part of an entire system of meaning governing the deployment of power. For Foucault, the eighteenth-century preoccupation with the body of the criminal contrasts with, but also parallels, the modern attentiveness to the convict's soul. The shift was from punishment to discipline, but it was not tantamount to a shift from physical cruelty to humanitarianism. It resulted rather from a recasting of the rules governing the effective deployment of power. Where in the Old

[86] I owe this point to Philip Benedict.

Regime it was assumed that the spectacle of prolonged and punctiliously orchestrated infliction of pain on the body served to broadcast the terrible cost of crime—and the sovereign's power to exact justice—by the mid-nineteenth century the logic of correction, which stipulated the reorganization of the criminal's whole mental disposition, cast the prison, not the scaffold, as the arena for the exercise of state power. For our purposes, what is most relevant in Foucault's analysis is his emphasis upon the spectacle of punishment, and especially the *supplice*, the infliction of pain on the body of the condemned, as the central feature of Old Regime justice.

As we have seen, the spectacle was indeed the thing. An execution was a "real-life theatre production with the gallows as the stage set, and the executioner, the condemned, the confessor and the escort as the *dramatis personae*."[87] Usually the scenario followed a predictable course: the ritual march to the scaffold, an exercise in shaming often combined with an amende honorable; the priestly exhortations and homilies on repentence; the victim's own confession and penitential words to the crowd; the often prolonged spectacle of death, sometimes accompanied by torture or mutilation; the victim's last words; and the deposition of the corpse and its subsequent decay or dismemberment, either in public or in the more private context of a surgical amphitheater. This scenario would be followed by an epilogue: the public discussion and evaluation of the execution, which sometimes found its way into print. Here, Barthès's diary itself served as one forum, albeit a semiprivate one, for this final account.

Foucault's emphasis on the spectacle of Old Regime punishment, based as it is on various eighteenth-century sources, thus finds confirmation in Barthès's diary. But while he cer-

[87] John McManners, *Death and the Enlightenment: Changing Attitudes to Death in Eighteenth-Century France* (Oxford, 1985), p. 387.

tainly acknowledges the contingent, unpredictable, even an-archic possibilities inherent in the staging of an execution—indeed, they are crucial for his larger analysis of the contradic-tion in the Old Regime system of criminal justice that led to its negation—his main protagonist, the focus of his analytical gaze, is, somewhat paradoxically, the passive body of the con-demned. Subjected to the supplice, which serves to inscribe its flesh with the crime itself, the body on the scaffold is con-fronted with the sovereign power of the monarch, and ulti-mately annihilated.

The evidence from "Les heures perdues" suggests two mod-ifications of Foucault's formulation. First, it really is not war-ranted to posit the supplice as the dominant feature of Old Regime executions, at least if one cares to acknowledge the quantitative weight of evidence. Only a minority of execu-tions in Toulouse between 1738 and 1780 entailed torture, mu-tilation, or some other punishment beyond the mere dis-patching of the victim; and while a substantial number were broken on the wheel, the vast majority perished relatively quickly at the end of a rope. Punishment did not normally fit the crime, at least not in the detailed, atrocious, sometimes absurd manner of marking the condemned's body with signs of the crime, as exquisitely described in *Discipline and Punish*. Of course, Foucault is not interested in quantitative evidence but in the logic of power, where a single emblematic case, like the extraordinarily prolonged and torturous execution of Da-miens, Louis XV's attacker, in 1757, is as convincing as an archive of examples.

If the supplice does not stand out in Barthès's account, nei-ther, then, is the body framed as the spectacle's focus. Rather, what emerges from his observations is something anathema to Foucault's antihumanist perspective, and somewhat surprising from a man who often looks upon those who mounted the scaffold as "monsters of nature." Not the *body* but the *person* is cast in the leading role. It is the victim, in all the fullness of his personhood—praying, pleading, speechifying, stoically resigned, defiantly resisting, or merely suffering—whom Barthès, perhaps unwittingly, presents in page after page of his diary. His descriptions of the condemned are sometimes detailed and specific with regard to physiognomy and demeanor: they are "robust," "very pretty," "old and ugly," "excessively fat," "of medium height," "impertinent," "docile," "obstinate," "pious," "tranquil," or the like. They go mad or resort to ruses. They have occupations, birthplaces, confessional identities, and even biographies. On occasion the scene on the scaffold inspires him to present a capsule morality tale as a sort of life-history conceit, as when twin brothers were hanged together for theft in 1773: "And so they lose their lives on the same day, attached to the same gallows, just as they first saw the light of day the same moment from the same woman."[88] On occasion too he and the crowd are moved by a victim's compellingly pious or noble comportment on the scaffold to acknowledge his (and their) humanity with their tears. The only other individuals in "Les heures perdues" to be accorded this recognition of their personal characteristics are the great and important men, from parish priests to the royal intendant, who so impressed our diarist. Not even the members of his family are endowed with such living traits.

Barthès's accounts of executions, as I have interpreted them, and Foucault's analysis differ primarily because of their radically different approaches to the experience. Barthès constructs it as a narrative, while Foucault anatomizes it in terms of the contradiction between the legal "trial" of the supplice and the public spectacle that it ultimately was. It is likely, then, that Barthès, in preserving the wholeness of the experience, reproduces it as it was viewed by his contemporaries,

[88] 704:197.

especially given the moralizing tone of his account. But even his observations give evidence of a contradiction that closely parallels, if it does not exactly reflect, Foucault's analysis. For the emergence of the condemned as a full-blown person in his account is made possible only by the theatrical frame of the execution itself, where the performative dimension created conditions at once rule-bound and unpredictable.

As spectacles or theatrical performances, executions usually proceeded roughly according to script. Rules and procedures ideally governed the rite. Arlette Farge goes so far as to assert that "the whole edifice of execution could only stand up if, based around it, there were a quasi-historic certainty that nothing could be allowed to impede it or divert it."[89] But, as Foucault and others have shown, and as we have seen, impeded and diverted it sometimes was; the ritual was subverted by mishaps and threatened by the unexpected. Indeed, spectators knew to expect the unexpected, sometimes outright disaster.[90] Would the victim physically resist his fate? Would he go mad? Would he destroy the gravity of the moment by uttering some rebellious or scurrilous remarks? Would the executioner botch his task? And would the executed man even stay dead? As we have seen, mishaps and eccentricities abounded in and around the scaffold. By its very nature the script was open to improvisation, constructed as it was in the course of the ritual through the interactions of executioner, victim, cler-

[89] Farge, *Fragile Lives*, p. 197.

[90] In an extremely interesting article on executions in Britain, Thomas Laqueur argues that the carnivalesque crowd was the "central actor," thus undermining the ritual's status as solemn state theater. "Crowds, Carnivals and the State in English Executions, 1604–1868," in *The First Modern Society: Essays in English History in Honour of Lawrence Stone*, ed. A. L. Beier, David Cannadine, and James M. Rosenheim (Cambridge, 1989), pp. 305–56. The evidence from Toulouse does not confirm this view, though it does suggest that rites of execution were open to great variety in their actual staging.

gymen, and sometimes the crowd. In this respect executions, though ritually configured in a prescribed manner, were far from formalized gestures. Instead, they offered the possibility of startling departures—a noble or vituperative speech, an exemplary or stoic death, a body that sputtered and writhed its way to death . . . The liminal space created by this rite of passage was, of course, fraught with mystery and danger. Perhaps this is what really attracted Barthès and those many Toulousains like him who regularly haunted the scaffold.

In turning now to other aspects of Toulouse's ceremonial life we should be alert to some of the same properties evident in the ritual of execution. For, as performance, all ceremony to some extent bears a dual nature: it is scripted, orderly, and formalized while remaining open to variation and improvisation, even to the point of breakdown or failure. And thus all ceremony reveals an essential tension between regimentation on the one hand and variation on the other. Indeed, I want to suggest that attentiveness to this tension is a necessary element in any analysis of ceremonial and ritual life, but especially in the case of public religious devotions, where one rite, the procession, prevailed over all others.

CHAPTER 4

PUBLIC
DEVOTIONS

*The eighteenth in the morning, the season being extremely dry
and the heat extraordinary, not having rained for more than
two months, the messieurs the capitouls made a vow to Our
Lady of the Daurade and having had sung a high mass in the
maison de ville they did the same at the Daurade where, after
having offered the Virgin their vow and the prayers of all the
inhabitants of the city, they had the image taken down from
its place above the altar at seven in the evening, the church
filled with people of every station to ask God by the intercession of his mother for a more suitable season for the preservation of the fruits of the earth, which are perishing before our
very eyes because of the extreme heat.*

*On Sunday the twenty-fourth of the same, all the religious
communities of the city, having assembled at two o'clock in the
afternoon in the church of the Dalbade, left in procession from
the said church after vespers with the image of Our Lady
under a magnificent pavilion and dressed in an extraordinarily rich robe; the* bailles *of the Confraternity of the Assumption
. . . bore the candles around the image, which was carried by
the children of the parish despite the opposition of the said*
bailles *who presumed to carry it. Then came the capitouls,
their assessors, and the whole bourgeoisie, everyone bearing a
candle. The procession was formed by a countless number of*

people of all stations. It made a station at Saint-Etienne and then returned by the street Croix-Baragnon to the Daurade where the image was honorably put back in its place, and with great devotion. She carried the vows of the city in her arms. The next Friday between six and seven in the morning an abundant rain fell without storm or wind.

"Les heures perdues," August 1738 (699:25)

WHILE IT IS a commonplace that eighteenth-century France was still profoundly Catholic, despite the Enlightenment, it might be claimed that Toulouse was unmatched among the realm's cities for public piety and popular fervor. This was the city, after all, that tried and executed Jean Calas, that Voltaire subsequently branded an outpost of fanaticism. This was a city still marked by its experience during the Wars of Religion when, as a Catholic bastion in a sea of Protestantism, it became the regional center for the Counter-Reformation. This was a city whose religious institutions ranged from the powerful office of the archbishop of Toulouse to the four penitential companies that bore the crusading Catholicism of the religious wars into the eighteenth century. And this was a city whose numerous and varied clergy exercised considerable influence over the laity. Barthès records that in 1738 the corpse of a Protestant woman was nearly dragged through the streets on the order of an angry parish priest who had failed to convert her on her deathbed. Only the fact that her husband had friends in high places prevented the priest from having this execrable deed carried out.[1]

As would be expected in such a city, many, if not most, of the ceremonies Barthès describes were religious in nature. He does not, of course, pause to note all the routine rites and devotions that filled the collective life of the faithful: the thousands of baptisms, marriages, and funerals that marked the life cycles of ordinary Toulousains; the masses that took place daily in each of the city's scores of churches and chapels; the countless religious processions that brought clergy and laity alike into the streets; or the preaching and evangelizing that seemed to be the speciality of a religious center such as Toulouse. These and other devotional ceremonies form the backdrop for his diary, the background noise, so to speak, of

[1] 699:3, 4.

ceremonial life in an Old Regime city. But Barthès does provide us with a view of more notable religious displays and rituals, enough for us to appreciate that, despite the changes in mentalité that were distancing some people from their faith, ceremony was still largely religious in nature.

Much of that ceremony dated from the period of the religious wars, a time not only of great civil strife and public fervor, but also of abundant creativity in the realm of religious ritual. Public life in eighteenth-century Toulouse still displayed marks of this creativity: it was still a Counter-Reformation city, combining demonstrations of baroque piety with the outdoor sociability characteristic of a meridional capital. Most Christian ritual—indeed most religious ritual—serves to commemorate the past, from the birth and death of Christ to the martyrdom of the saints. But many local rituals precisely made a point of preserving the memory of the Wars of Religion, a particularly traumatic period in Toulouse's history. One such ritual was the annual procession staged on Saint Roch's day, when the capitouls and the chapter of the Daurade marched to the Minime convent on the city's outskirts.[2] The procession, which also attracted legions of the faithful, dated to 1587 when the city, then afflicted by an epidemic, made a vow to Saint Roch to secure the patron of plague-sufferers' protection. Although the plague was the immediate pretext for the new procession, its real stimulus was the overheated devotional climate of the late 1580s, when the forces of Catholic militancy were rapidly gaining ground in the city. In the much cooler atmosphere of the late eighteenth century the procession continued to be mounted—proof that the Old Regime rarely disgarded anything in the way of ceremony.

Perhaps the most prominent bearers of the Catholic militancy forged during the religious wars were the four peniten-

[2] 699:195.

tial companies of Toulouse. These brotherhoods of laymen and clergy—known as the Blue, Black, Gray, and White Penitents by the color of the hooded robes, or *cagoules*, they donned for their meetings and processional outings—were all founded in the mid-1570s and played an important role in stimulating popular piety in the last decades of the religious wars. By the eighteenth century the penitents had largely given up the public displays of mortification that had been a hallmark of their devotions; the Blue Penitents even took to wearing shoes when they processed. The four companies also seem to have experienced a decline in membership. But they were still capable of reviving the religious fervor that gave rise to their founding. This fervor was at no time more apparent than during the Calas affair, when the White Penitents ostentatiously escorted the body of Calas *fils* to his final resting place, claiming this "nouveau convertis" as an honorary member of their company.[3]

As a dutiful and fervent member of the Gray Penitents, Barthès dwelt on his confreres' activities in his diary, naturally giving pride of place to his own company. Hardly a public devotion took place in the city without the participation of the hooded penitents; they were all-purpose celebrants. Often their ritual contributions were quite novel, displaying a flare for the dramatic that had been a feature of their ceremonial since the sixteenth century. The Grays celebrated the octave of their patron, Saint Jean, in 1750 with a procession that included music as well as a rhythmically coordinated, almost choreographed march of the penitents in which half waved censers while the rest strewed flowers along the route.[4] During the Corpus Christi festivities in 1751, the Grays appeared in the streets with five children, outfitted as saints and accompanied by lambs, in tow.[5] In September 1754 the canons of the

[3] 703:57. [4] 699:329–30. [5] 700:30.

Trinity invited both the Blues and the Grays to participate in a procession celebrating the freeing of twenty-six slaves purchased from Morocco for six thousand livres each. The penitents came out in force, each walking hand in hand with a child dressed as an angel.[6]

Like many religious orders, the penitential companies specialized in certain devotions and holy figures. They were particularly avid sponsors of the cult of relics, having been endowed with several important sacred remains over the years. In 1756 the Blue Penitents received a piece of the true cross along with a relic of their patron, Saint Jerome, as a gift from the pope, a donation they celebrated in the company of the other penitential brotherhoods and several religious orders with special masses, processions, and other festivities.[7] The Gray Penitents' chapel, dedicated to Saint Vincent, whose remains were on display, was a center of popular fervor. In July 1775, Barthès reports, two supplicants, a young man severely crippled with rheumatism and a paralyzed woman, were miraculously healed while praying to the saint. Both left their crutches behind them in the chapel. Barthès praised this divine intervention as a blow against the fashion of "Pirronism [sic]" that too often has "served to ridicule his Almighty power."[8]

One of the most regular of the penitents' devotions was their pilgrimage to Notre Dame de Garaison, located in the foothills of the Pyrenees in the region of Tarbes. This Marian shrine had long been a popular gathering spot for supplicants to the Virgin, and it had been the chosen site of the penitents' only extramural devotion at least since the early seventeenth century. (The Gray Penitents supposedly began the custom in 1604 to pray for the health of Henri IV.)[9] Barthès reports,

---

[6] 702:32. For a similar example from Paris in 1725, see Farge, *Fragile Lives*, pp. 174–75.

[7] 702:74.   [8] 705:74.   [9] 699:125.

however, that the pilgrimage had not been carried out since 1674. And it was only in 1743, on the occasion of the Blacks' excursion to the shrine in September, that he notes it as a regular feature of penitential ceremonial. Thereafter the companies individually staged their processional sorties every seven or ten years. On these occasions the penitents would gather early in the morning for prayers at their chapel, march to a city gate, and, accompanied by crowds of well-wishers including members of the other companies, set off on the journey to Garaison. The entire pilgrimage normally took about eight days, during which, chanting hymns and reciting prayers, they offered an edifying sight to onlookers along the route. In 1778 the Gray Penitents carried with them a large silver medal struck on one side with the image of Notre Dame de la Pitié and on the other with a portrait of the king and queen: the procession that year was dedicated to the queen's health. Six children marched among the thirty-eight Grays who participated in the pilgrimage.[10] When the penitential pilgrims returned to Toulouse, they would be greeted by the City Watch, the three other companies, and large numbers of the faithful. The homecoming was also the occasion for additional devotions, such as special masses and Te Deums, as well as celebrations of various sorts, including fireworks and the firing of muskets.

The penitents' regime of processions demonstrates that the crusading zeal so evident during the religious wars—and which harked back to the origins of this collective rite in earliest Christian times—still lived in the eighteenth century. To proselytize to the faithful, to instruct and preach to the masses, was a burden assumed by several religious groups, not only the penitents. At least three religious orders, the Jesuits, the Fathers of the Christian Doctrine, and the Fathers of Saint

[10] 705:166.

Rome, regularly undertook extended missions lasting up to three weeks in the city itself. These occasions were veritable religious campaigns designed to shore up the populace's faith. When the Jesuits encamped in the suburban parish of Saint-Michel in May 1758, they confronted many peasants from the countryside and therefore preached in Occitan in order to be understood.[11] The mission of the Fathers of the Christian Doctrine at Saint-Sernin began in late April 1770. Performed every ten years, it resulted from an endowment left by a canon of the basilica. Its closure on May 27 was marked by a procession of children, students, widows, the capitouls, and the preaching fathers. The children marched carrying instruments of the Passion, while the young men walked barefoot. At the end of the ceremony, as was the case for every mission, the fathers planted an iron cross to commemorate their successful evangelizing campaign.[12]

Viewed in terms of ritual display, the Wars of Religion were more than a distant memory to eighteenth-century Toulousains, for they were repeatedly revived through a variety of processional rituals. Moreover, these revivals served to define the city by evoking this traumatic but ultimately triumphant episode from its past. One ceremony more than any other was responsible for keeping alive the spirit of the religious wars in eighteenth-century Toulouse. This was the general procession staged annually on May 17. It was on that day in 1562, after a three-week struggle, that the city's beleaguered Huguenots succumbed to the assault of the combined forces of Catholic soldiers and armed citizens. Their violent expulsion was thenceforth celebrated every year as the "deliverance of the city" with a general procession and other public devotions. In

---

[11] 702:127.

[12] 704:15; 701:42–43; 705:105; 706:27. For missions in Provence, see Michel Vovelle, *Les métamorphoses de la fête en Provence de 1750 à 1820* (Paris, 1976), pp. 72–74.

1762 the celebration—dubbed by Voltaire "the procession to thank God for four thousand murders"—was one of the great moments in Toulouse's history, commemorating the two-hundredth anniversary of this glorious event. It was a lavish spectacle, attracting, according to Barthès, thirty thousand tourists and pilgrims. And its popularity was enhanced by the renewal of a papal bull originally issued in 1564 granting the faithful indulgences for attending prayers at either the cathedral or the Basilica Saint-Sernin. Barthès's excitement was matched only by his prolixity.

It had been raining heavily for several days leading up to the celebration, so much that the capitouls feared that they would have to postpone the procession. But midday on May 17 the downpour suddenly stopped and the proceedings began posthaste. The procession set off from Saint-Sernin with the city's religious orders and communities leading the way, each under its banner and cross, followed by the eight parish delegations. Next came the ninety craft corporations. Four-man teams of craftsmen were assigned to bear the basilica's forty-nine holy relics, each team escorted by four other co-workers carrying candles and another four holding torches. The chapter of Saint-Sernin followed, holding aloft the relic of the holy crown along with a gold heart that the capitouls had ritually presented to the canons of the basilica the previous evening. Next marched the capitouls, each carrying a candle, followed by the officers of the Hôtel de Ville and the corps of militiamen making up the Watch. A crowd of people took up the end of the procession, which made its way across the city to the cathedral, where mass was said. Afterward the participants reassembled, joined by the indigent inmates and the directors of the Hôpital de la Grave, and, along with a group of pilgrims, returned to Saint-Sernin. Tapestries decorated the streets all along the procession's route, their elevation mandated by the capitouls on pain of a one-hundred-livre fine.

The solemnity and decorum of the day's festivities did not prevent contention in the procession's ranks, however. On the return march to Saint-Sernin, the regiments of Bearn and Berry, currently billeted in the city, suddenly claimed the right to carry the dais bearing the Holy Sacrament. The capitouls traditionally were granted this honor, but the troops insisted that the privilege was theirs wherever they were garrisoned. Neither party would give way, and the procession remained stalled in its tracks while the parlement deliberated on the justice of the respective cases. After a half hour of discussion, the sovereign court ruled in favor of the capitouls and the procession continued on its course.

Fireworks were scheduled for the evening of May 17, but the torrential rains and flooding forced their postponement. The first of June provided a break in the weather, and the celebration picked up where it had left off two weeks earlier. But so too did the quarrel over precedence between the capitouls and the royal regiments. Having been rebuffed by the parlement in their attempt to seize a place of honor in the general procession, the troops now claimed the privilege of lighting the fireworks, a privilege, naturally, designated to the capitouls. The regiments even threatened to occupy the plaza to force the issue. Eventually—Barthès does not tell us how—the capitouls prevailed in the quarrel and the celebrations continued untroubled.

The Place Royale, the large square in front of the Hôtel de Ville only recently constructed, was the central stage of this phase of the festivities. Barthès's description of its splendors runs to several pages; it would be tedious to recapitulate it in detail here. But it is important to appreciate the dimensions of the festive offering, especially its propagandistic and didactic features, for it combined entertainment with edification. Indeed, one of its more striking aspects is its richness in language: Latin phrases, mottoes, and scriptural quotations graced the fireworks' scaffolding on every facade. Near the base was inscribed a poem alluding to the struggle against Calvinism that the May 17 procession commemorated. "Religion graced and defended this place with its illustrious and precious blood," it read—a reminder that it was on this very spot two hundred years earlier that the Huguenots had met their bloody doom. "It is here that faith triumphed wondrously. Calvin, seeing this, shuddered. . . . The relics of the saints are Toulouse's honor." Higher up on the scaffolding—designed as a Temple of Religion—another set of texts proclaimed the virtues of the true and only faith. "The Faithful believer will find here his only entrance. . . . Harmony and peace reign in this place. . . . Those who are excluded perish without help. . . . This way, and by no other, one ascends to heaven." Still higher, the four church fathers, Saints Gregory, Augustine, Jerome, and Ambrose, stood on the corners of the temple, each statue captioned with a Latin inscription. For example, Saint Gregory was "The Father of Christian morality," Saint Augustine "The Son and defender of grace." At the summit of the structure language becomes sparse, as if there were now only a simple truth to proclaim, one needing no rhetorical embellishment. Indeed, the temple's four penultimate facades were each graced with a single word, "Religioni." A statue adorned the structure's peak: "Religion" holding a chalice in one hand and a cross in the other, crushing underfoot the prostrate figure of Calvin himself.

The festive display thus spoke to the populace, or at least to that portion capable of decoding its Latin inscriptions. Like the mass, which some people understood as a liturgical text while others followed as merely a series of ritual gestures, the Temple of Religion proclaimed the message of militant Christianity in both word and symbol, allowing the educated and uneducated alike to gaze upon it comprehendingly, though in somewhat different ways. The very structure of the display also spoke in two different keys. The temple itself was classical in form, an architectural monument composed of symmetrically positioned steps on each of its four sides leading upward to a series of antique urns placed on each corner; and four columns, constructed of materials intended to give the appearance of veined marble, on each side. It was a "temple," not a church: a classical structure, with all its well-known associations from antiquity, appropriated to serve in the celebration of militant Christianity. Those Toulousains who considered themselves cultivated, who were in the know concerning the rising cult of neoclassicism in mid-eighteenth-century France, could thus look upon the structure and take pleasure in the fact that such a religious and civic exercise was at least in good taste. But the edifice was a temple in symbol only; in actuality it functioned as a platform for the fireworks that terminated the May 17 festivities. In this respect it appealed to the masses: both the peasants, pilgrims, and tourists who flocked to Toulouse for the occasion and the thousands of townspeople who gathered in the Place Royale. As much as the occasion was an edifying religious celebration, the fete's crowning feature was pure entertainment.

These celebrations were unique in Toulouse's history, probably the largest demonstration of public faith ever staged in an eighteenth-century city. As David Bien has suggested,[13] they were emblematic of the atmosphere of anti-Protestantism that allowed for the prosecution and execution of the Calvinist Jean Calas that same year. But Barthès's diary enables us to appreciate that Toulouse's public life was periodically marked by great religious festivities which, while not as large as either the May 17 celebrations in 1762 or the secular fetes that will be discussed in the next chapter, were still impressive, and undoubtedly stimulated popular fervor and piety.

---

[13] Bien, *The Calas Affair*, pp. 48–55.

Several of these were in honor of saints. The cult of saints was supposedly on the wane in post-Tridentine France, but devotion to such holy figures and their relics remained strong in eighteenth-century Toulouse. Devotion was especially enthusiastic when it came to the canonization of near-contemporary holy figures or those associated with a particular religious order. In April 1738, the canonization of two saints, Vincent de Paul and the Jesuit François Regis, plunged the city into an extended period of celebration. The ceremonies in honor of Vincent de Paul began on the twelfth and lasted eight days; virtually every religious order, church chapter, and penitential company got into the act, each staging processions and celebrating masses, some offering musical homages. The Gray Penitents had a symphonic Te Deum performed in their chapel. Each evening throughout the octave of celebrations the hospital Hôtel-Dieu was illuminated with candles and bonfires while rounds of artillery charges were detonated from the banks of the Garonne.[14] The city barely had a chance to catch its breath from this nonstop series of fetes and devotions when celebrations for Saint François Regis began on April 27, leading off with festivities at the Jesuits. In succeeding days other religious orders, colleges, churches, and confraternities honored the new saint with their own processions and devotions. On April 28, the chapter of Saint-Etienne, in the company of the Jesuits, processed through the city, while the City Watch fired their muskets at every station. The ceremonies climaxed with a final celebration at the Jesuits and a fireworks display.[15]

Similar ceremonies for either the canonization of saints or the beatification of candidates for sainthood took place on at least five occasions during the period Barthès observed his city.[16] On one of these occasions, when the Cordeliers cele-

[14] 699:9–12.   [15] 699:14–17.
[16] 699:44, 241–42; 701:4; 704:42–43, 102.

brated the elevation to sainthood of eight brothers martyred in South America, the festivities were complemented by a small outbreak of miracles in the city, so great was the fervor aroused by the devotions.[17]

The fervor was just as great for relics of saints and martyrs for the church. Toulouse had been known for centuries for its treasures of relics, especially those in the crypts of Saint-Sernin, reputed to be one of the holiest places in all of Christendom.[18] While officially sponsored devotion to these relics seems to have diminished in the eighteenth century, the city's religious orders and confraternities continued to maintain the cult of relics, especially when they were in their possession. On two occasions the bodies of saints were translated to Toulouse from Rome as a gift from the papacy. During the octave celebrating the Gray Penitents' reception of the remains of the third-century martyr Saint Vincent in 1762, the festivities were on a grand scale. Because he was a Gray Penitent himself and obviously brimming with pride at this boon to his company's prestige, Barthès gives a particularly full account of the extended celebrations.

The Grays' chapel was the center of the festivities. From the capitouls' storehouse of ceremonial accoutrements, the penitents borrowed two large, freestanding portals, which they placed face-à-face on either side of their chapel's main entrance; an embroidered cloth was stretched between these towering gates, thus creating an atrium in the street to serve as an impressive entry leading into the chapel's interior where the saint's remains were to be displayed. This "vestibule" was furnished with tapestries, tableaux, escutcheons of the city's chapters and religious communities, and flags of four artisan confraternities. Biblical quotations and other decorations

---

[17] 699:242.

[18] On the Saint-Sernin relics, see Schneider, *Public Life in Toulouse*, pp. 102–4.

dressed the chapel's interior. After an inspection of the coffer containing the pope's gift—which included the saint's head, an arm, a few vertebrae, and some dried blood—by a team of physicians and clergymen, the remains were displayed to the faithful. Then commenced the usual round of processions: the capitouls and the Watch, the other penitential companies, and most of the city's religious orders all making their way to the Grays' chapel to offer their prayers and homages to the new relics. These were staged every day over the course of the octave. The celebrations climaxed with a large-scale cavalcade honoring the new relics. In the company of the capitouls, the Blue Penitents, and the musicians of the city, the Grays paraded the coffer across the city, their route covered with tapestries and flowers. The people's enthusiasm was great, noted Barthès. During the octave six hundred masses were performed in Saint Vincent's honor and seven thousand people took Holy Communion. In the course of the main procession a miracle reportedly occurred: a Gray Penitent, a crippled artisan, suddenly threw down his crutches and walked unaided. On several evenings the devotions were followed by more profane celebrations—banquets at the Grays' chapel and fireworks. The last night of the octave the penitents had a symphonic Te Deum performed in their chapel.[19]

Gifts from the pope, these relics demonstrated Rome's ability to extend its influence over the religious life of this distant French city. Never was this influence greater than during Jubilees, those periods of special devotions ordered by the papacy, during which people could earn extraordinary indulgences. Jubilees were celebrated in Toulouse in six different years between 1738 and 1780: 1745, 1751, 1759, 1762, 1770, and 1776. In 1745 the Jubilee originally intended for Italy alone was extended to France at the request of Louis XV to celebrate his recent recovery from illness.[20] The 1751 Jubilee on the oc-

[19] 703:90–99. [20] 699:204.

casion of the Holy Year attracted thousands of the faithful from throughout the region, who flocked to Toulouse to partake of the devotions that only a great religious center, with its cathedral, religious orders, and massive processions, could offer.[21] The Jubilee of June 1759 lasted three days. The devotions at the Jesuits, which included nonstop preaching, special conferences, and meditations, were especially popular. Barthès notes that many people even managed to attend prayers scheduled at two in the morning in the Jesuits' chapel.[22] The Jubilee of 1776, one offered by the papacy every twenty-five years, overwhelmed the city for the better part of a month, from the end of June to the end of July, during which there were processions daily in the late afternoon by different religious orders, parishes, and confraternities. Barthès, perhaps exaggerating, claimed that the large procession at Saint-Etienne was followed by a cavalcade of fifty thousand people.[23]

The papacy's influence over local ceremonial life must have provoked the resentment of some lay people and clergy of Toulouse, a city under the aegis of both a Gallican Church and a parlement suspicious of ultramontane tendencies. But, as we have seen, local religious figures and institutions were not without ceremonial resources: they too could create moments of heightened public devotion. Among them was the archbishop of Toulouse who, although usually absent from the city, as was the norm for such great prelates, still managed to assert regularly his ceremonial prerogatives. For example, every ten years the archbishop visited a selection of churches to offer the Eucharist to communicants and to perform the sacrament of confirmation as well. Barthès's first record of this extraordinary ceremony is in March 1755, when the archbishop appeared in different churches on successive Sundays. Under the banner and cross of their parishes the faithful pro-

---

[21] 700:24. [22] 702:157. [23] 703:103–4.

cessed to the church in which the prelate was conducting the mass.[24] In 1768 he administered the sacrament in the cathedral to the parishioners of Saint-Sernin, du Taur, Saint-Michel, and Saint-Pierre in the morning, and at the church of the Dalbade to those from the Daurade and Saint-Nicolas in the afternoon.[25] Lominie de Brienne—the churchman about whom Louis XVI supposedly quipped when his appointment to high ecclesiastical office was proposed, "Shouldn't an archbishop at least believe in God?"—created a stir when he broke with tradition in 1775 and reserved his sacramental attentions to children under the age of seven.[26] On such occasions the confluence of people from throughout the city, drawn to receive the sacrament from the archbishop's own hands, was enormous. These were ceremonies that momentarily transformed the city into a truly Christian community, when, at the same time, in one place, and through the gesture of one man, thousands of its inhabitants partook of the central Christian mystery.[27]

Not all public devotions were carefully planned and orchestrated events. All too frequent were the hastily mounted, often massive supplicatory processions staged in the face of some natural or man-made disaster—fire, flooding, or drought. As we have seen, Toulouse regularly suffered from these collective calamities. Indeed, except for a modest improvement in the city's fire-fighting capabilities, the populace was still woefully ill-equipped to deal with various ravages. Thus, like their forebears, they turned to prayer. There was, however, a choice of supplicatory measures before the populace and clergy, a choice indicative of the variety of intercessors and devotions available to Catholic supplicants in moments of need.

The most time-honored and popular measure was to pray for the intercession of the Black Virgin at the parish church of the Daurade. This three-foot-high image of Mary was of Byz-

[24] 702:43–44.
[25] 704:72–73.
[26] 705:43–45.
[27] See also 703:35.

antine origin dating from the fifteenth century. When drought or flooding threatened, or when a fire raged, people and clergymen alike often turned to her in prayer. Sometimes the Virgin would merely be taken down from the altar, allowing the faithful to pray and make offerings before her. When the danger was particularly grave or prolonged, the municipal authorities would make a vow to the Virgin, dress her in a new robe, and parade her about the city. Such devotions took place in August 1738, during a long drought. The Black Virgin, newly bejeweled and robed, holding in her arms a paper bearing the city's "vow," was carried through the major thoroughfares by a group of children of the Daurade parish.[28] If a "miracle" occurred, and the rains came to end the drought, as was the case three years later as well as in 1775, another procession was staged to thank the Virgin for her intercession.[29] Sometimes, in the case of flooding and fire, the Virgin would be hastily snatched from the Daurade altar and brandished before the threatening fire or swelling waters.

Emergency processions might be mobilized at any hour. When the Garonne's waters threatened to crest in May 1765, the priests of the Saint-Nicolas parish, chanting litanies and ringing bells, marched to the river's banks at midnight "to implore the aid of divine mercy."[30] Two years earlier, the relics from Saint-Nicolas were borne in procession across the Pont-Neuf and dipped into the flooding waters.[31] In 1743 it was the Carmelites who marched to the river, prayerfully supplicating an end to its torrents. Bearing an image of the Virgin, they also tossed a scapular into the water for good measure.[32] Such a materialistic approach to the efficacy of certain devotions was not unique. A fire behind the church of the Dalbade in September 1752 was met with a brigade of marching Carmelites who threw a scapular into the blaze—which, recorded

[28] 699:25–26. [29] 699:83; 705:64. [30] 703:188.
[31] 703:79. [32] 699:118–19.

Barthès, "immediately died down."[33] Other religious orders were also prepared to rush out at all hours to appease a conflagration with their prayers and special devotions.

The range of supplicatory measures at the populace's disposal was impressive. The Dalbade church offered the Black Virgin; the Benedictines, their long iron cross; the church of Saint-Nicolas, its relics; the Carmelites, the scapular; the Fathers of the Trinity, another sort of cross; Saint-Sernin, its storehouse of relics—all utilized, at one time or another, to combat fire, flooding, or other collective misfortunes. In moments of prolonged or extreme danger to the entire populace, however, the city marshaled its combined devotional resources into action. In 1768, during a four-month drought, the capitouls asked the vicars-general to order public prayers: each parish, each religious order, and both hospitals performed two processions daily.[34] When the city was suffering from a long drought compounded by widespread sickness in 1771, there were supplicatory processions performed by all the city's religious orders, parish churches, and lay confraternities; even cloistered nuns processed behind the walls of their convents; relays of processing orders and confraternities traversed the city daily, marching between the Cathedral Saint-Etienne and the Basilica Saint-Sernin. The Holy Sacrament was exposed in every church and chapel; and the forty-hour orison was also observed.[35] The same repertoire of devotional exercises was ordered on several other occasions, most notably during the long crisis of the animal distemper epidemic in 1774.[36]

Although the Catholicism of city-dwellers was not as enmeshed in the rhythm and vicissitudes of nature as that of peasants, there was at least one ceremony in Toulouse which ritually dealt with the elements on an annual basis. Predictably, given the city's dependence on and occasional victim-

[33] 701:21.   [34] 704:75–76.
[35] 704:161.   [36] 705:39, 84–85.

129

ization by its main waterway, it had to do with the Garonne River. Each spring on Ascension Day, the Benedictines in the company of the city's fishermen would march to the banks of the Garonne, embark on a boat, and row out to the Ramier island. There they would ceremonially dip a long metal cross into the river's waters to ensure their fecundity and calm. Sometimes, especially when the river was turbulent, they would forgo the boat ride and perform the ritual from a bridge. Barthès avidly followed the ceremony, noting his disappointment those years when disputes between the monks and the fishermen thwarted its execution. When the ceremony was reestablished in 1761, after a seven-year hiatus caused by a particularly bitter dispute, it was staged with added éclat. Crowds of people clambered upon boats to accompany the monks and fishermen to the Ramier; others lined the river's banks. The ceremony was performed to the accompaniment of beating drums and music. The neighborhoods adjacent to the island celebrated the pious event with festivities and illuminations.[37]

Most of these ceremonies had a civic as well as a religious dimension. Public devotions, they also mobilized elements of the populace and officialdom alike in exercises that gave expression to the urban community. When emergency processions were staged in face of fire or some natural disaster, the lives and property of the city's inhabitants were at stake. When the May 17 general procession took place each year, it celebrated not only the triumph of the true faith but a historic victory for Toulouse. Celebrations honoring a religious order or penitential company's reception of holy relics also honored the city that now harbored them. As in any other Catholic city, religious festivities largely ordered Toulouse's official calendar. And on a material level Toulouse's commerce de-

[37] 703:160.

pended greatly upon the spending habits of a steady stream of pilgrims and tourists drawn to the provincial capital to witness its many devotional displays.

The capitouls participated in most religious ceremonies, indicating by their presence that the city's devotional life was a civic, as well as a spiritual, concern. They also appropriated religious rituals as a means of enhancing their own prestige. Tradition warranted, for example, that newborn children of current capitouls would receive the spiritual kinship of the town councillors. All of the father's seven colleagues would stand as the child's godparents, giving him (in the case of a boy) their names. The child would also receive a gold medal struck with the city's emblem. Fanfare and celebrations preceded the baptismal ceremony itself; the Watch, to the accompaniment of music and the firing of muskets, escorted the child, his parents, and the capitouls in procession to the parish church.[38] Similar ceremonies accompanied another very public baptism under the aegis of the capitouls' spiritual guardianship, that of converted Jews. There were only a handful of resident Jews in eighteenth-century Toulouse, for this stronghold of Counter-Reformation Catholicism was barely hospitable to Calvinists, as the Calas family found out to its misfortune, let alone Jews. Of those Jews established in the city, several apparently considered conversion the best modus vivendi among their Catholic neighbors.[39] On at least five occasions in the 1760s and 1770s the capitouls, again serving as godparents, escorted a "New Christian"—once a whole

[38] 699:4; 704:62; 703:III; 704:20–21.

[39] The capitouls attempted to regulate the presence of Jews in the city in the eighteenth century, and especially to limit Jewish merchants to a single month each season for conducting business. All Jews had to register with the authorities upon their arrival and give notification of the date of their departure. In 1729, the capitouls issued an ordonnance which stipulated that Jewish merchants would be allowed in the city for the months of January, April, July, and October only. Archives munipales de Toulouse, GG 789: "Ordonnance en execution des règlements faits contre les juifs."

family of them—dressed in a white robe, to the baptismal font. Like a capitoul's newborn, the convert was presented with a gold medal, a sign that the city was sponsoring his or her baptism. And again there were processions, music, military salutes, and crowds of people to witness the edifying event. Barthès was among them, barely containing his glee that the church had claimed an errant soul for the true faith. When a five-year-old boy, "pretty as a picture," was presented to the baptismal font, the diarist noted with relief that his youth prevented him from "having been imbued with the principles of Rabbinism."[40]

The largest collective devotions in Toulouse were also civic exercises, since they gave ritual expression to the urban community, its integrity and hierarchy. These were the general processions, the massive parades that momentarily transformed the city into a religious stage, its inhabitants into actors in a perambulating pageant. The city's ceremonial calendar was punctuated by four annual general processions: those on Corpus Christi Day, Pentecost, the Feast of the Immaculate Conception, and May 17. Most years there were also occasions for extraordinary general processions, when, for example, a dignitary died or the urban community gathered to supplicate heaven for relief from drought, flooding, or other such natural disasters. The rains that came in April 1775 ending a two-month drought were celebrated with a general procession that bore the Black Virgin through the city.[41] The funeral ceremonies for deceased royalty included elaborate general processions with many of the participants draped in black crepe as a sign of grief.

What distinguished a general procession from other processional displays was not only its size, but, more importantly, its inclusion of virtually the entire range of the urban community, from artisans and a delegation of the hospital poor to

[40] 703:16–18; 704:47; 705:59.   [41] 705:64.

high churchmen and parlementaires. The point of the ceremony was to assemble in a coordinated fashion the city as a whole, or at least those elements that had a corporate, official identity. It was, however, as Robert Darnton has noted, only one version of the social structure, one, moreover, that "exaggerated some elements and neglected others."[42] Indeed, the portrait of the city presented in the general procession was largely an archaic one fixed sometime in the sixteenth century. While additional elements, such as new religious orders or corporations of officials, were included in the ceremony as they were created, the terms of inclusion did not apply to all sorts, especially not to those who lacked a corporate identity. In Geertz's terms, the general procession was less a faithful "model of" the urban community than a "model for" an ideal version of what it once was.

Despite its supposedly inclusive and comprehensive design, the general procession varied its cast of participants and organizational structure from occasion to occasion. It is unlikely that one could ever decipher precisely the meanings behind these variations. What did it mean, for example, that there were three contingents of 150 of the city's poor at the funeral procession for the queen in 1768, and only two on the occasion of the king's in 1774—that the queen was known as a patron of the poor? These battalions of indigents, incidentally, seemed to serve as boundaries between different elements of the official community, marking, for example, a transition in the procession from the religious orders and artisan corporations (who usually led off the parade), to the municipal officials (who occupied its middle position), to the royal officers and other legal types (who took up the end). For the general procession commemorating the two hundredth anniversary of the expulsion of the Huguenots in 1562, the sequence bespoke

---

[42] "A Bourgeois Puts His World in Order," in *The Great Cat Massacre*, p. 122.

the religious significance of the moment: the city's religious orders both led and closed the parade. But for this and many other general processions, some of the ritual's focus at least was on the icons, relics, or the Host itself borne aloft by the marching participants, thus reminding us that these were essentially religious rituals whose ultimate meaning lies as much in the fervor they were meant to arouse as in the sociology of their organization. The participants attentively eyed the order of precedence as they processed, but they also presumably lifted their gaze from their ranks to acknowledge the spiritual significance of their collective presence.

BARTHÈS's diary provides us with one of the most complete portraits of public religious life in an eighteenth-century city. To be sure, there are gaps and omissions in his account. For example, one would like to know more about the devotional exercises of craft confraternities, or to be provided with more detail about particular religious ceremonies, such as the Corpus Christi processions. But there is sufficient detail and richness to assemble a repertoire of religious ceremonies, which I have done here, as well as to draw some conclusions about public devotions in an eighteenth-century metropolis. Beyond the extraordinary frequency with which Catholic ritual punctuated the lives of city-dwellers—and if nothing else, Barthès's diary stands as an effective refutation of the assumption that public devotion drastically waned in the eighteenth century— what other insights does the document provide?

One evident feature is the scale of public devotions. Many processions and ceremonies, especially those performed by individual confraternities and religious orders, involved merely a handful of confreres or priests. But others, especially those that attracted Barthès's attention, were massive, crowded spectacles, drawing a confluence of clergymen and ordinary people. General processions always entailed a great outpouring of people and institutions; so too did the elevations of saints' relics, the consecrations of ecclesiastical buildings, and other devotional exercises, both planned and spontaneous. Some people undoubtedly attended these spectacles and rituals out of mere habit or curiosity. (As is said: who can resist a parade?) But Barthès also allows us to appreciate the level of popular fervor that these events evoked. Sometimes he merely observes that the people were deeply moved by a priest's preaching, or marvels at the solemnity and decorum exhibited during a certain procession. A fervent believer himself, Barthès certainly wanted to believe that popular devotion matched his own. On other occasions, however, his comment is more pointed: as mentioned, he notes the occurrence of miraculous healings during three different mass rituals; and he also relates that during the celebrations for the canonization of a saint at the Jesuits, many people roused themselves from their beds to attend devotional services at two o'clock in the morning. When supplicatory processions were staged in the face of a natural calamity, the fervor of the people, mixed with desperation and hope, was obvious. The devout Christian, too often relegated to the margins of eighteenth-century history, occupies center stage in the pages of "Les heures perdues."

But the people's fervor was not entirely spontaneous. For Barthès's diary also demonstrates the centrality of another feature of public devotional life in the Old Regime: the importance of the regular clergy in sponsoring particular devotions, organizing religious rituals, and generally stimulating the populace's piety. To the mobilizing efforts of such orders as the Jesuits, Franciscans, and Dominicans should be added the public exercises of Toulouse's four penitential companies, for these also strove to heighten popular fervor and draw the masses into the streets. The parish clergy was, of course, the most important element in ordinary people's devotional regime: it was they who normally said the mass, heard confession, celebrated the Eucharist, and offered the other sacraments for most churchgoers (although people could also choose to receive the sacraments from regulars). In the wake of the Tridentine church's insistence on parochial discipline, the parish provided the basic cell-structure of lay piety; and here the parish clergy presided. But for extraparochial devotions and many, if not most, of those that were public in nature, the regular clergy often took the initiative. It was they who frequently organized emergency supplicatory processions, championed the cults of saints and relics, formed the largest contingent in the general processions, missionized to the faithful; and it was in their convents and monasteries that the holy images and relics were to be found that attracted the populace's fervor. The monastic life was increasingly under attack in the eighteenth century, both by the philosophes and by more benign critics of the church. But while the numbers and influence of the regular clergy may have been declining, their presence was still imposing in such a metropolis as Toulouse. And this at least insured that whatever trends were working to undermine the strength of popular faith would find a formidable counterweight in a corps of ecclesiastics dedicated to shoring it up.[43]

Most of the devotions Barthès describes took place outdoors, or at least entailed a procession as a preliminary or ancillary part of the ceremony or ritual. Indeed, most of the devotions *were* processions. These two features are so obvious as to seem banal. Commonplace in the pages of "Les heures

[43] Jacques Chiffoleau has warned against seeing the procession as a spontaneous rite among the laity, noting the importance of the regular clergy in mobilizing the laity in fifteenth-century Paris: "Les processions parisiennes de 1412: analyse d'un rituel flamboyant," *Revue Historique*, no. 575 (July–September 1990): 37–76. To acknowledge the importance of the regular clergy in sustaining popular piety is also to suggest that when the religious orders waned in number and influence, especially with the Revolution, the people's faith thus lost a crucial support.

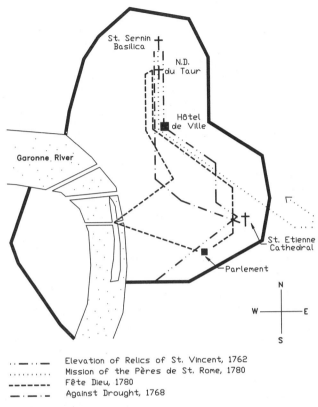

St. Sernin
Basilica

N.D.
du Taur

Hôtel
de Ville

Garonne River

St. Etienne
Cathedral

Parlement

N

W——|——E

S

. . — . . — Elevation of Relics of St. Vincent, 1762
. . . . Mission of the Pères de St. Rome, 1780
— — — — — — Fête Dieu, 1780
— . — . — Against Drought, 1768

Routes of Four Processions in Toulouse

perdues," processions were even more common in the actual
streets of eighteenth-century Toulouse. I have suggested that
we think of those myriad processions not mentioned by Barthès as the background noise of the city's ceremonial life. That
such processions were daily events is probably an understate-
ment. The city's ninety craft corporations each processed several times yearly, as did its twenty-five religious orders, eight
parish churches, and thirty or so lay confraternities. Each of
the several secular corps of officials also had its calendar of

devotions that included periodic processions. To these must be added the large-scale processions and the confluence of processing institutions, both ecclesiastic and secular, that marked major holy days, as well as the impromptu processions staged in moments of danger. Every time a priest was called to minister to a dying parishioner, the Holy Sacrament was borne through the streets in procession. Finally, literally thousands of burial corteges traversed the city, for every body was carried to its final resting place in procession.[44]

How to understand this commonplace of public devotion? How to see it as more than a banality of religious life in the Old Regime? First, we should not assume that because processions were ubiquitous and frequent they meant less to the faithful who participated in them, or to observers. After all, the same could be said of the mass. That popular fervor and enthusiasm often attended religious processions is abundantly clear from the pages of "Les heures perdues." They even could occasion miracles. Moreover, these rituals often drew upon the participation of large numbers of city folk who in this respect played an active role in the devotional and civic life of their city. This civic dimension of ceremonial life should be emphasized, because it was in taking to the streets in procession that many ordinary people, who otherwise had no place in the urban hierarchy, participated in the process by which the city ritually constituted itself. Indeed, it would not be going too far to claim that these rituals composed a gestural constitution—a ritual projection of the fundamental and timeless elements of a particular urban order.[45]

[44] On the importance of processions in civic life, see, among many studies, Bernard Chevalier, *Les bonnes villes de France du XIVe au XVIe siècle* (Paris, 1982); and Moshe Sluhovsky, "'Ora Pro Nobis Beata Virgo Genovefa': The Public Cult of Sainte Geneviève" (Ph.D. diss., Princeton University, 1992).

[45] For a meticulous exposition of this notion in another context, see Muir, *Civic Ritual in Renaissance Venice*, chap. 5.

It would seem therefore that the procession expressed not "communitas" but "structure"—or rather an ideal image of the city's structure.[46] While daily street life was disorderly and promiscuous, processions and other outdoor devotional ceremonies usually proceeded in a relatively structured fashion. In a great ceremony such as the general procession, the city got "dressed up," was put in order: it was an occasion when the ideal of a society both hierarchical and harmonious, both stratified and unified, attained a momentary reality. And it was then that the city as a corporation, an ideal social order, lived. Of course, this civic ideal also had a spiritual meaning, for it was in public devotions such as processions that the unified church, the body of Christ, took form.

The structured aspect of the procession suggests an approach to ritual that has found favor with a number of anthropologists: a focus on the formalized quality of most ritual as a key to its power, symbolic meaning, and social function.[47] Indeed, it is the highly formalized nature of ritual behavior that distinguishes it, in this view, from other activities—a distinction which suggests Durkheim's fundamental division between the sacred and the profane. Ritual's formalization is evident in several ways. It usually relies upon repetition: words, gestures, songs, dances, and the like repeated, sometimes obsessively, but in any case in a preordained and usually codified manner. It thus follows that ritual is a highly rule-governed activity. Like certain linguistic codes, it also is an expressive mode characterized by condensation or compression, rather than a more expansive, prolix, or varied expression of a colloquial sort. Finally, ritual usually creates a space re-

---

[46] Ronald Grimes, *Symbol and Conquest* (Ithaca, 1976), pp. 66–69, argues against the *communitas* model in analyzing religious processions in contemporary New Mexico.

[47] Bloch, *Ritual, History and Power*, Tambiah, "A Performative Approach to Ritual," pp. 123–66; Roy Rappaport, "The Obvious Aspects of Ritual," in his *Ecology, Meaning, and Religion* (Richmond, Calif., 1979), pp. 173–221.

moved from everyday activities; it evokes an appropriately special form of etiquette among participants and observers alike,
usually referred to as reverence; and, like a theatrical performance, it is temporally delimited, with a clearly demarcated
beginning and end.

These characteristics hold more than an aesthetic interest.
For it is in its formalized nature that some anthropologists
claim to have discovered the essence of ritual dynamics.
Moore and Myerhoff, for example, emphasize ritual's "tradi-
tionalizing role" derived precisely from its formal properties:

> In the repetition and order, ritual imitates the rhythmic
> imperatives of the biological and physical universe, thus
> suggesting a link with the perpetual processes of the cos-
> mos. It thereby implies permanence and legitimacy of
> what are actually evanescent cultural constructs. In the
> acting, stylization and presentational staging, ritual is
> attention-commanding and deflects questioning at the
> time. All these formal properties make it an ideal vehicle
> for the conveying of messages in an authenticating and
> arresting manner.[48]

Similarly, S. J. Tambiah argues that since the purpose of ritual
is usually to affirm "constructs . . . to be taken on faith and
considered immutable, then it is a necessary corollary that the
rites associated with them be couched in more or less fixed
form, be transmitted relatively unchanged through time."
Thus "conventionalized," ritual has the added result of psy-
chically distancing both participants and observers from its
potential emotional effects. Tambiah understands ritual in
this sense as "simulations," "engaging not raw emotions but
'articulated' feelings and gestures."[49] In Susan Langer's terms,

---

[48] Sally F. Moore and Barbara G. Myerhoff, "Introduction: Secular Ritual," in *Secular Ritual* (Assen and Amsterdam, The Netherlands, 1977), p. 8.
[49] Tambiah, "A Performative Approach to Ritual," pp. 131, 146.

ritual is not a "free expression of emotions but a disciplined rehearsal of right attitudes."[50] And for the most part, these attitudes are "congenial to an ongoing institutionalized intercourse."

Among anthropologists who focus on ritual's formal properties, Maurice Bloch has been responsible for sharpening this focus most critically. For him, most ritual is not only formalized, but thereby restricted in its expressive capacity. Like religion in general, ritual is semantically "impoverished"; it is "a language where many of the options at all levels of language are abandoned so that choice of form, of style, of words and of syntax is less than in ordinary language." Ritual cannot explain or even engage reality; it is (in Bloch's terms) "arthritic," a "one-way street," yielding only a single pattern of meanings and allowing only fixed, predetermined responses. The dead hand of tradition not only stifles expression in the rituals it causes to be reenacted; it also removes to a realm beyond criticism and scrutiny the interests and powers that sustain it. In evoking the analogous dichotomy between ordinary and formalized language for his analysis of ritual, Bloch has essentially reproduced the Marxist distinction between knowledge and ideology, as he readily acknowledges.[51]

Allowing for some overstatement inherent in such abstract formulations, I think we can recognize many of these features in the processional regime that dominated public devotions in our eighteenth-century city. First, while processions could vary considerably, they were essentially variations on the same theme. Indeed, it was precisely the stock nature of the procession that made it a dependable feature of public ceremony,

[50] Susan Langer, *Philosophy in a New Key* (Cambridge, Mass., 1951), p. 123–24; quoted in Tambiah, "A Performative Approach to Ritual," p. 133.

[51] For Bloch's views, see "Symbols, Song, Dance and Features of Articulation: Is Religion an Extreme Form of Traditional Authority?" in *Ritual, History and Power*, pp. 19–45; and idem, "The Past and the Present in the Present," *Man*, n.s., 12 (1977): 278–92.

easily mobilizing a populace that was well-versed in its dynamics.[52] The sameness that all processions shared endowed the ceremony with its spiritual appeal: now as ever Christians marched to testify to their faith. Just as Toulousains in the sixteenth century had militantly defended their church against the heretics, so their eighteenth-century descendants marched again and again in public witness to that same church. This sameness also asserted an allegiance to traditional values and beliefs in the face of a rapidly changing world and city. But, conversely, this sameness meant as well an unyielding and limited ceremonial repertory, which necessarily constrained the range of expression in public life. And yet the eighteenth century was a period when public sociability found new outlets. In some respects social interaction was freer, more accommodating to the expanding vistas of the eighteenth-century city; in others it exhibited a tendency to conform to the growing split between popular and elite milieus. There is some evidence that participation in general processions began to wane in the eighteenth century.[53] If so, it is likely that this stemmed in part from a growing perception that traditional, unbending church ceremony could not accommodate itself either to the dynamics of urban life or to contemporary tastes.[54]

---

[52] Of course, just because rituals remain unaltered does not imply that their meanings cannot change. On this, see David Cannadine, "The Context, Performance and Meaning of Ritual: The British Monarchy and the 'Invention of Tradition,' c. 1820–1977," in *The Invention of Tradition*, ed. E. Hobsbawm and Terence Ranger (Cambridge, 1983), pp. 101–64.

[53] For evidence on this, see *Public Life in Toulouse*, pp. 302–3.

[54] Relevant here is the current discussion over the eighteenth-century public and how it embodied new types of sociability and represented a new ideal of interpersonal communication that stood in contrast to dominant, traditional forums in the Old Regime. I discuss this issue in the context of new festive forms in the Conclusion. Here I would add that a consideration of the procession in the context of this discussion might clarify what seems to be some confusion over what precisely we should understand as the antonym of "the public." The tendency seems to be to think of it as "court

This leads, in turn, to a second way in which the procession was a limited or constrained ritual: its relatively fixed social composition. While some processions, most obviously general processions, enlisted thousands of participants, even these excluded many other townspeople. It excluded them not only because many had no place in the corporate community, both religious and secular, that the ceremony's ranks predominantly reflected, but also because these ranks had largely remained unchanged since the sixteenth and seventeenth centuries. Thus, the newer elements of urban society—most crucially the growing merchant community, but also the numerous unorganized workers as well as visiting royal troops—had no place in the general procession. Unlike Renaissance Florence, where elasticity seems to have characterized the very nature and social composition of public ceremony,[55] in eighteenth-century Toulouse public devotions, at least, preserved their archaic, timeless quality, even at the cost of excluding large elements of the social order.

But to see the procession in such terms is only to view it in

---

culture" or "absolutist culture" (see, for example, Sarah Maza, "Women, the Bourgeoisie, and the Public Sphere: Response to Daniel Gordon and David Bell," *French Historical Studies* 17, no. 4 [Fall 1992]: 948). This, however, places excessive emphasis on the center as determinant of the dynamics of eighteenth-century political culture. A more precise conceptualization of the dominant structures of eighteenth-century culture is in terms of corporatism, which comprehends in its scope everything from the academies to the guilds, and captures as well precisely that restrictive and formalized aspect of Old Regime culture to which the emerging notion of the public was supposedly opposed. As a ritualized expression of a corporatist vision of society, the procession was thus quintessentially traditional in its form yet also, perhaps, no longer capable of expressing the social and cultural dynamics of contemporary society. On corporatism, see especially the work of David Bien, for example, "Offices, Corps, and a System of State Credit: The Uses of Privilege under the Ancien Régime," in Baker, *The Political Culture of the Old Regime*, pp. 89–114.

[55] Trexler, *Public Life in Renaissance Florence*.

a rarefied light, detached from the context of its actual enactment.[56] From Barthès's diary, however, we can appreciate that the procession also embodied a fundamental tension between the rules that ideally governed its staging and the actual behavior of its participants. And this is where the performative aspect of the ritual is apparent. For, among other things, a procession was a performance. It was akin to a theatrical production, with individual participants having assigned roles, the ensemble bent on presenting a coordinated display. In this sense it was designed to proceed without variation time and again according to script. But the formalized arrangment of the procession could also be shattered by the participants themselves. For as in any "live" performance, there was a risk that participants would fail or refuse to perform as scripted or even that they would improvise their own script. In particular, the risk was that certain parties would fall out over issues of precedence.

Indeed, we saw an example of such fractious behavior in the general procession in May 1762, when royal troops disrupted the proceedings with their claim to occupy a place of honor in the ceremony. From Barthès's diary we learn that processions "broke down" in like fashion with some regularity. The capitouls interrupted the annual procession for Saint Roch in 1738 to force the members of the Confraternity of the Assumption to remove their hats in the town councillors' presence.[57] In December 1742, during a procession of the Confraternity of Our Lady of the Daurade, held on the eve of the Feast of the Conception of Our Lady, an altercation erupted between the parlement and the capitouls because the magistrates refused to allow the town councillors to sit with them in the Daurade's

[56] This indeed is one of the criticisms of an approach to ritual that focuses exclusively on its formal features. See the critique of Bloch's views by John D. Kelly in the *Journal of Ritual Studies* 5 (1991): 133–35.

[57] 699:24.

choir.[58] The four penitential companies, supposedly united in a common regime of devotional severity and militant faith, often were at odds over matters of precedence and privilege. The failure of the Whites and the Blacks to show up for the processional convoy for President Maniban in 1762 was just one example of how their feuding led to conspicuous breaches in ceremonial etiquette.[59] There was, in short, ample ground for some anxiety about the proper staging of a procession, and for a sigh of relief when the performance came off successfully.[60] Barthès gives voice to this concern when he remarks on the decorum and order of a particular processional display.

Thus, like other performances, a procession entailed risk— a risk that was obviously well worth taking, considering what was, both socially and spiritually, at stake. In Mervyn James's well-turned phrase: "Conflict was the dark side of the moon of unity. However, without conflict, no social wholeness either."[61] In the realm of ceremony as elsewhere, a risk incurred

[58] 699:105.   [59] 703:105–8.

[60] Other conflicts occasioned by processions in eighteenth-century Toulouse include: a contest between the capitouls and the chapter of Saint-Sernin over the latter's refusal to bear the relics from the basilica during the May 17 general procession in 1708 because of the weather, a conflict that necessitated the postponing of the ceremony (Rosoi, *Annales de la ville de Toulouse*, 4:627); two conflicts over precedence, involving the Blue Penitents, the capitouls, and the chapter of Saint-Etienne, during the funeral procession for the dauphin in 1712 (ibid., p. 641); a dispute between the prévôt of Saint-Etienne and the capitouls during entry into the cathedral on the occasion of a Te Deum service in 1719 (ibid., Supplement, p. 18); a conflict between the confrères de la Sainte-Epine and the capitouls during the Pentecost procession in 1758, which ultimately was resolved in court (ibid., p. 145); a dispute over the placement of the capitouls in the May 17 general procession in 1784, which caused a halt in the procession's progress for over a quarter of an hour until the parlement could deliberate (Archives départementales, Haute-Garonne, C 288).

[61] Mervyn James, "Ritual, Drama and Social Body in the Late Medieval English Town," *Past and Present*, no. 98 (February 1983): 4. It seems to me, however, that James misinterprets the procession as an instance of Turner's *communitas*. For while wholeness and unity were certainly ideas that the

and surmounted yields a greater sense of success than would be possible if risk had never been an element of the performance in the first place. And it is in this sense that the procession could escape the formalization and "inarticulateness" that Bloch posited as features of most ritual. For the participants themselves could make the idiom of the procession more articulate than its form would lead one to expect. Like play, in Huizinga's understanding of the notion, "tension" and the uncertainty of an activity's "coming off" were fundamental elements in the procession's dynamic appeal.[62] Processions were in this sense like executions, where the preordained end-

---

Corpus Christi procession strove to realize ritually, it cannot be said as well that differences were dissolved or suspended, an essential ingredient in the liminal experience. Rather James is more on the mark when he stresses "creative tension" and the dialectical relationship of unity and difference that the ritual embodied. But this is not the same as *communitas*.

Edward Muir has argued that Renaissance Venetians' willingness to risk socially embarrassing conflict in staging frequent processions reveals "not so much a lack of concern for the image of the republic as the overwhelming importance [they] granted the concept of ceremonial primacy." *Civic Ritual in Renaissance Venice*, p. 202.

Mary Ryan, in her study of parades in three nineteenth-century American cities, argues that a special quality of this form of ceremony was that it prevented the conditions of contention among participants. She writes, "The genius of the parade was that it allowed the many contending constituencies of the city to line up and move through the streets without even encountering one another face to face, much less stopping to play a specified role in one coordinated pageant." As interesting as this argument is, much of her evidence suggests that in reality the nineteenth-century parade was just as susceptible to contention and withdrawal as the procession. Mary Ryan, "The American Parade: Representations of the Nineteenth-Century Social Order," in *The New Cultural History*, ed. Lynn Hunt (Berkeley and London, 1989), pp. 131–53. The quotation is on p. 137.

[62] Johan Huizinga, *Homo Ludens: A Study of the Play Element in Culture* (Boston, 1950), pp. 47–48. Of course, one might respond that many rituals which manage to "come off" with regular success exhibit no such tension— indeed seem to depend upon an untroubled, dependable, and tranquil execution as the source of their appeal. And the most relevant rite in this respect is the mass, whose very predictability and sameness—from church to

ing was still subject to the vicissitudes that haunted the progress to the scaffold. And tension indeed characterized the procession, as it marched the conceptual line between prescribed regimentation and the risk of disorder, between the humdrum and the improvised, between a routine ritual and a ritualized occasion for popular fervor.

In turning now to a range of political festivities, among the questions we will want to keep in mind is whether they too were marked by this crucial tension, and if not, what this might have meant for the ceremonial life of our eighteenth-century city.

---

church and even from country to country—is still a comfort to the faithful. I can only respond with the observation that the procession should perhaps be seen as a counterpoint to the mass—a ritual distinguished by lay activism and by the performative aspect of uncertainty, both absent in the mass, and thus elements that explain its appeal as a ritual complement to the clergy-led, church-based liturgy.

CHAPTER 5

POLITICAL FESTIVITIES

The second of this month at eleven in the morning, the messieurs of the parlement, on the order they received from the court, left from the palace, all the chambers in a body, in red robes and preceded by their ushers, and went to Saint-Etienne where messieurs the capitouls with the officers of the city had assembled with the Watch under arms, beating drums, [with] oboes and trumpets, to have sung the Te Deum as an action of thanks to the Lord for the taking of the city and county of Nice from the king of Sardinia by Monsieur the prince of Conty and the infant Dom Philippe and for the prosperity of the arms of France and Spain in Italy. . . . In the evening there were bonfires in all the streets of the city and illuminations in the windows of the houses.

"Les heures perdues," June 1742 (699:144–45)

ALTHOUGH THE weight of ceremony was still largely religious in the eighteenth-century city, the church held no monopoly in the realm of ceremony in the Old Regime. Political culture was rich in ritual expressions, from royal entries, coronations, funeral processions, and *lits de justice*, each an important element of the monarchy's symbology of power, to the myriad ceremonies mounted regularly by lesser or local institutions.[1]

There were, of course, important differences between church and secular ceremonies. One difference was that religious ritual most often focused on holy figures or animated crowds of believers in devotional exercises, while political ceremony usually centered on officials or powerful men. Indeed, it is striking to observe that despite the corporate nature of the Old Regime hierarchy, individuals, not institutions, commanded the most ceremonial attention in the city. This is at least the view one gets from Barthès, who displayed a tendency to mythologize men of position, transforming everyone from parish priests to the king into a paragon of virtue and wisdom. If one were to rely solely upon his diary for an understanding of the nature of authority in the Old Regime city, one would have to conclude that it was important individuals—veritable "big-men," from local officials to royal agents and great noblemen—who wielded power.[2] But sometimes

---

[1] These, however, have been mostly studied in the context of the period before the eighteenth century. Ralph Giesey notes the virtual disappearance of one royal ceremony, the royal entry, and the modification of another, the *lit de justice*, arguing that this reflected a turn away from a legally based, ceremonially constituted monarchy to one where the ritualized figure of the king ruled "absolutely" from his enclosed domain of Versailles. On this see especially "The King Imagined," in Baker, *The Political Culture of the Old Regime*, and idem, *Cérémonial et puissance souveraine*. Despite these important transformations, I will be arguing that representations of royalty were nevertheless common on the local scene.

[2] In borrowing the concept of the big-man from anthropology, I want to emphasize that even officials in Old Regime France seemed to require that

the populace itself indicated by its actions that it too recognized the authority of such men. On the evening of January 4, 1743, for example, a fight broke out between a bailiff's son and a peasant. The crowd that gathered managed to put a stop to the altercation but, more to the point, promptly escorted the two combatants to the house of the first president of the parlement, who was then asked to interrogate them and decide which should be imprisoned.[3]

In fact, presidents of the court commanded singular respect and deference, which placed them well above their corporate confreres, at least ceremonially. The recovery from an illness of President Bastard in March 1739, for example, was celebrated like a royal triumph. The Carmelites solemnly feted the occasion with a mass and the singing of a Te Deum, a rite normally reserved for the monarch. Elsewhere in the city various festivities continued throughout the day and into the night. The corps of musketeers fired rounds of volleys, while fountains gushed forth gallons of wine for the populace's delectation. In the evening a large fireworks display was set off from an elaborate scaffold depicting the figure of "Health" surrounded by three goddesses spouting Latin phrases of

---

their "bigness" be demonstrated and celebrated in ostentatious ceremonies, usually entailing great expense and lavish, seemingly pointless, display. There was, in other words, an element in the cultural expectations surrounding such elites that went beyond the ex officio, and which really cannot be explained in vestigial terms—as a remnant of feudalism, for example. Clearly, elites competed with one another in the ceremonial and festive displays they mounted, and this too was a "big-man" element of their comportment. I realize that as originally formulated by Marshall Sahlins, big-men, unlike chiefs, usually stood outside the governing structure, and in this sense my use of the term is somewhat inaccurate. See Marshall Sahlins, "Poor Man, Rich Man, Big-Man, Chief: Political Types in Melanesia and Polynesia," *Comparative Studies in Society and History* 5 (1962–1963): 285–303; and Karen Ericksen Paige and Jeffrey Paige, *The Politics of Reproductive Ritual* (Berkeley and Los Angeles, 1981), pp. 223–26.

[3] 699:109.

thanksgiving and homage. In sponsoring these celebrations—Bastard undoubtedly paid at least some of the expenses—the president was encouraging the populace to look upon him as a man of singular importance and munificence. When he was elevated to the position of first president in 1762, Bastard received honors befitting a local kinglet. (His marriage, it must be noted, to a relative of Madame de Pompadour did not hurt his standing.) His entrance into Toulouse on November 7 was in the grand processional tradition; streams of people met his entourage, and the city greeted the new first president with gifts, illuminations, and fireworks. The citywide celebrations in his honor continued throughout November and into December, including fireworks, public dancing, private dinners, and balls, with the Hôtel de Ville festooned with edifying tableaux and emblems.[4] In 1770 it was Bastard's wife and family's turn to be feted with fireworks in the Place Royale and a great dinner in the Hôtel de Ville to which the "Ladies of the City" were invited.[5] When Bastard died in 1777 at ninety-four, by then the doyen of the parlement, his body lay in state first at the Cordeliers' convent and then at the general hospital, where it was visited by all the city's religious orders in procession.[6]

The first president of the parlement was, along with the archbishop of Toulouse, the most important man in the city. But on a ceremonial level he had rivals of various sorts. Other "big-men" loomed large on the local scene, especially scions of prominent families who added high positions to their inherited wealth and renown. Perhaps the most powerful family in the region was the Riquet clan, the descendants of Pierre-Paul Riquet, the late-seventeenth-century financier whose ingenuity and resources were largely responsible for the construction of the Canal du Midi. In the eighteenth century the Riquets

---

[4] 703:113–15.   [5] 704:129.   [6] 705:141.

continued to exercise proprietary rights on the canal and still obviously commanded considerable respect in the city. Thus, in February 1750, when a member of their clan, Riquet-Bonrepos, arrived to take up the position of *procureur général,* he was accompanied by a cavalcade of 120 uniformed soldiers, armed with sabers and dressed in his family's colors.[7] When in 1758 Riquet-Bonrepos's daughter married President Riquet, a scion of another branch of the family, the celebrations took a novel form. Separate brigades of workers and domestics in their employ assembled, draped in the colors of their patrons, and marched in procession to the newlyweds' country estate in Castelmaurou to escort them to Toulouse in the additional company of the maréchaussée.[8] When Riquet-Bonrepos's sister-in-law, a Maupeou, was named abbess of the Saint-Claire convent in the diocese of Narbonne, her benediction took place in the Black Penitents' chapel. The region's nobility was in attendance and the solemn event served as an occasion for concerts, private dinners, and other celebrations.[9]

The prominence of such families as the Riquets also carried obligations, among them a willingness and a capacity to offer both the populace and notables various entertainments and spectacles as testimony to their munificence and taste. That offered to the city in July 1739 by the comte de Caraman, another Riquet and the chief proprietor of the canal, was a veritable big-man display. The canal itself was the scene of a boat tournament in which contestants attempted to retrieve a hat placed atop a greased pole. The winner received a gold medal and forty écus. That evening, at a house owned by one of the count's employees on the banks of the canal, Caraman threw a dinner party and ball for the notables of Toulouse, who dined and danced within the illuminated hôtel while specially constructed fountains running with wine and a barge

[7] 699:319–20.   [8] 702:129–30.   [9] 701:50.

mounted with a fireworks display entertained those ordinary people who gathered without.[10] A year later, to celebrate his wife's birthday, the count invited several hundred Toulousains to a dinner party and concert at his hôtel in the Place Saint-Georges. Then again, while the "people of condition" supped within, the common people were not entirely forgotten: fireworks were provided to amuse the crowds that gathered in the plaza.

The Riquets clearly made a point of ceremonially flaunting their importance, but royal officials and other agents of the crown could command ritual allegiance from the city as a matter of right. When the intendant Saint-Priest arrived in Toulouse in 1753, he was met by the capitouls and in the course of his visit received the homage of a stream of local officials.[11] Three years later the town councillors feted his wife and daughter with a grand ball at the Hôtel de Ville.[12] But no one was lavished with more ceremonial attention than the duc de Richelieu, the commander for the king in the province of Languedoc. Richelieu visited Toulouse for the first time in 1741 and his sojourn occasioned citywide festivities lasting nearly three weeks. The duke was greeted by an honor guard composed of a train of uniformed corps, including a company of one hundred volunteers, eight companies of the *guarde bourgeoisie* of one hundred men each, four companies of merchants outfitted as military men, the maréchaussée of the province, a troop of the duke's domestics, his fifty guards, the City Watch, the *corps de la ville*, and several carriages. His route through the city traversed its major thoroughfares in the manner of a general procession, stopping at the cathedral for a Te Deum in his honor, and culminating at the archbishop's palace, where he was to reside during his prolonged visit. On May 30 the municipal officials feted the duke with a dinner at the Hôtel de Ville and a fireworks display in the Place Royale. On June 3, Richelieu again processed through the city, this time stopping at the sénéchal, where a group of students regaled him with panegyric speeches. The next day it was the turn of the Bourse des Marchands to honor the duke with a Te Deum and symphony at the Augustines' convent. That night he dined at the comte de Caraman's, who also provided fireworks in the square in front of his hôtel. On June 10, Richelieu visited the municipal college, where he was again harangued by the students in French, Greek, and Latin. And again, fireworks were set off in his honor. Although many of these events were reserved for the city elite of officials and notables, the populace, as was the rule in such festive moments, shared in the outdoor amusements. On this occasion, the large Place Saint-Etienne was covered with sand to allow for nightly dancing.[13] One would think that Richelieu had his fill of ceremonial attention from Toulouse after this three-week visit in 1741, but his capacity, or need, for expressions of homage was apparently endless. For when he returned to the city barely seven months later and was not greeted with what he considered to be sufficient ceremonial éclat, he severely reprimanded the capitouls for neglecting their duties. Thenceforth—in 1750, 1754, 1759, and 1766—whenever he even got near Toulouse he was punctiliously regaled with ceremonial honors.[14]

The question of ceremony often exercised the authorities. What was the appropriate ceremony, in kind and scale, to offer a visiting official or dignitary? At stake was not only the visitor's honor and a fear of offending him; the city's honor and reputation were on the line as well. For it must never be said that Toulouse failed to demonstrate the requisite politesse and savoir faire when it came to ceremonial offerings. As in

[13] 699:75–82.   [14] 699:321; 702:3–4, 169; 704:23.

social interactions between individuals, etiquette was a constant concern for collective bodies in the Old Regime, particularly provincial cities keen to conform to the ways of Paris and Versailles. Usually ceremony was dictated by tradition and precedence. Thus, a new archbishop was always presented with twelve candles of white wax and twenty-six jars of preserves on the occasion of his first entry into the city.[15] Sometimes visiting dignitaries would be asked what kind of ceremonial greeting they preferred. When the emperor of Austria passed through Toulouse in 1777, he made known in advance that he desired no festivities.[16] Other dignitaries carried out their visits "incognito," thus avoiding the attentions that an officially recognized sojourn would have necessitated. At least once a visitor's preference was deliberately ignored. In 1776, the duc de Chartres, the king's cousin, was making a tour of the realm's seaports. Beseeched by the capitouls to include Toulouse on his itinerary, he consented to a visit but stipulated that no ceremonies be staged in his honor. The municipal officials went all out anyway, carpeting the major thoroughfares, providing illuminations and other delights for the duke's eyes, only to have him arrive so late and in such a hurry to depart the next morning that he barely caught a glimpse of the display.[17]

The ceremonial attention lavished on these important individuals might seem somewhat paradoxical in a political order where the dynamics of rule were so notoriously impersonal and bureaucratic. But the paradox merely reflects the ritual dynamics established under Louis XIV. For it was then that a shift from "state ceremonials," in which the king played an active role, to "court ritual," where he was merely the sedentary and largely passive focus of punctilious attention, signaled the bureaucratization of royal power "operating normally and

[15] 703:2.   [16] 705:133.   [17] 705:99.

civilly, rather than remotely and capriciously."[18] While many local dignitaries and other magnates clearly attempted to command the same sort of ritual attention evident at Versailles—styling themselves as mini–Sun Kings—it is clear as well that they continued to play an active role in older ceremonials, most notably the ceremonial entry, that survived on a local level. But for what I have called the "big-man" displays mounted by local luminaries, there were even earlier antecedents. One was the type of munificence routinely practiced by feudal lords as proof of their generosity and worthiness as protectors. Favors of this sort, however, normally benefited a lord's immediate entourage, clientage, or subject peasantry. The other harks back to antiquity and indeed was more in keeping with a civic context: the custom of "euergetism," incumbent upon oligarchs in classical Greece and Rome, which mandated the dispensing of largesse in the form of festivals, banquets, games, buildings, and the like.[19] What was singular about this sort of munificence was not so much that the dispenser honored himself in the mirror of his generosity—the same, after all, could be said for any kind of patronage—but rather its civic dimension insofar as it was always dispensed to the city as a whole. And this was also characteristic of the types of festivities that local dignitaries frequently offered to the populace of Toulouse. Could these big-man displays have reflected, not simply conspicuous consumption recast as munificence, but also a desire on the part of eighteenth-century notables to define themselves in terms of classical ideals?

In any case, a procession of dignitaries visited Toulouse in the years that Barthès kept his diary, from great noblemen and

[18] Giesey, "The King Imagined," in Baker, *The Political Culture of the Old Regime*, pp. 41–59; quotation from p. 56. See also Sarah Maza's astute remarks in her article "Politics, Culture, and the Origins of the French Revolution," pp. 710–11.

[19] Paul Veyne, *Bread and Circuses: Historical Sociology and Political Pluralism*, trans. Brian Pearce (London, 1992).

king's ministers to provincial officials and foreign princes, most requiring a ceremonial greeting from the city. One bigman was conspicuously absent from the scene, however—the biggest of all. The last monarch to enter Toulouse was Louis XIV in 1659. In June 1777, the king's brother did visit the city, and his sojourn evoked a large ceremonial effort in his honor, including a daylong competition among boatmen on the Garonne, as well as the usual fireworks, illuminations, private dinner parties, and public dancing. But the last two Bourbons never felt obliged to visit the provincial capital. Like other dignitaries, however, the king periodically made a display of his munificence, even from the distance of Versailles. In 1752, to celebrate the birth of the duke of Burgundy, a royal order offered dowries of one hundred livres each to poor girls between the ages of fourteen and thirty wishing to marry. In November the royally sponsored mass wedding took place in the chapel of the Hôtel de Ville, with each of the fifty-six couples escorted to the altar by a capitoul. Afterward the newlyweds were treated to a dinner and ball. The next day they could return to receive their one hundred livres and complimentary marriage contracts.[20] The king had been good to his people.

IF THE monarch himself never visited Toulouse in the last century and a half of the Old Regime, symbolic and festive expressions of monarchical power abounded nevertheless. In fact, the royal family and the crown's interests and activities marked public life in the eighteenth century more than in any earlier time. The reign of Louis XIV may have been the summit of absolutism—certainly the ritual attention on the monarch reached its apogee at the Sun King's Versailles—but it was under the last two Bourbons that royalism projected its image and interests most effectively throughout provincial France.

[20] 701:19–20, 23–26.

Foremost, at least in terms of numbers, were the rituals to celebrate royal military victories. France, of course, was at war with various European powers during much of the time Barthès kept his diary. And local readers of the newspaper the *Gazette de France*, Barthès among them, were supplied with long accounts of the royal troops' progress. But the general populace also was kept abreast of France's fortunes on the battlefield. Indeed, since the seventeenth century there was a repertoire of "ceremonies of information," discussed and analyzed by Michèle Fogel in her book of that title, which broadcast to the public the vital facts of France's military victories (never defeats).[21] The populace hardly needed these ceremonies to remind them that their country was at war: periodic conscriptions, increased taxes, and food shortages were reminders enough.[22] But the ritual transmission of war news not only provided a triumphant ceremony to sugarcoat the often difficult conditions caused by the crown's military adventures; it also often conveyed rather precise information about particular battles—enemy towns seized, victorious generals, and the like.

In short, the successes of the king's armies regularly found an echo in Toulouse, and in other provincial cities, through a ceremonial avenue well established by the last part of the eighteenth century. The scenario was usually the same each time. The archbishop of Toulouse (or some other high official) received a letter from Versailles informing him that a particular enemy stronghold had been taken by the king and his generals and ordering the city to mount the appropriate ceremonies. The news was then "published" in the city: announced by the

---

[21] *Les cérémonies de l'information.*

[22] And so were the forced donations from the citizenry toward financing the royal war effort. In November 1759, placards appeared in the streets demanding that people bring their silver plate to be melted down for the "Needs of the State" (702:173–74).

Watch in the major thoroughfares, to the sound of trumpets and drums, and posted in several central locations. The ceremonial routine almost always included illuminations at the Hôtel de Ville, and usually at the homes of notables, bonfires, and sometimes fireworks. In June 1739, when the celebrations feted the conclusion of a peace with Portugal, the city's religious orders were threatened with a fine if they failed to illuminate their convents and monasteries.[23] The essential part of the celebration, however, that which gave it its solemn air, was the singing of a Te Deum in the cathedral in front of the capitouls and parlement, who were ordered by the crown to attend.

The *Te Deum laudamus* is a hymn to the Almighty and a confession of faith, a chanted prayer dating from the late fourth century, which entered the liturgy two centuries later. Church historians have documented the intricate process during the Middle Ages by which it became associated, both in the empire and in France, with the secular power.[24] Suffice it to say that by the late fourteenth century it came to play a central role in the French coronation ceremony, sung in honor of the newly crowned monarch. "It thus signified a hymn of recognition of a king who now had no superior save God. It was the moment of his apotheosis," writes Michèle Fogel.[25] Under Henri III the hymn underwent a further mutation: detached from its previous contexts of mass and coronation, it was then and thereafter sung alone to solicit God's grace or celebrate royal triumphs, especially on the battlefield.

This is indeed its main association in the eighteenth century. The Te Deum was chanted on at least seventy-two occasions in Toulouse during the period covered by Barthès's

---

[23] 699:43.
[24] This literature is summarized in Fogel, *Les cérémonies de l'information*, pt. 2.
[25] Ibid., p. 160.

diary, usually in the Cathedral Saint-Etienne. Some of these marked religious events or honored church officials; the first president Bastard also enjoyed the rare privilege of having a Te Deum sung in his honor upon his recovery from illness in 1739. But as the accompanying list indicates, it was a ritual reserved primarily for the king, his family, and the fate of his armies (see table 4). Half the occasions were in celebration of a royal victory or the declaration of peace. In such manner, the military campaigns of the king's armies in the far-flung corners of Europe were brought home to the people of Toulouse. War thus governed the very rhythm of local celebration, forcing the city to react ceremonially according to the pace of battle. The later months of 1745, for example, were an especially crowded time, as French armies pursued their campaigns in the War of the Austrian Succession on the Dutch and Italian fronts. The third of June the Te Deum marked the taking of Fontenoy; July 14, the submission of Tournai. August 8, Ghent capitulated to the French, provoking the usual Te Deum. News reached Toulouse of the fall of Bruges on August 17, an occasion feted not only with a Te Deum and the usual illuminations, but also with a bonfire that the capitouls lit and then circled three times. Afterward fireworks were set off in the Place Royale. The twenty-fifth of August another Te Deum signaled victory over Oudenaarde, and five days later in Sardinia. The next month the capitouls and magistrates again assembled at the cathedral for a Te Deum to celebrate the fall of Dendermonde in Flanders. The taking of Ostende provoked an outbreak of Te Deums in various Toulouse churches on September 20, as well as the usual pyrotechnic displays in public spaces. The next week more Te Deums marked military successes in Nieuwpoort and other places in Flanders. On October 20 the hymn was sung for royal victories in Parma and Piacenza in Lombardy, and five days later for the successful campaign in the Piedmont. On November 3, the usual ceremonies planned to celebrate the recent victory

TABLE 4
Te Deums: 1738–1780

Date	Occasion
March 1739	Health of first president
June 1739	Peace
July 1739	Beatification
February 1741	New archbishop
June 1741	Entry of duc de Richelieu
May 1744	Health of king
June 1744	Military victory
July 1744	Military victory
July 1744	Military victory
August 1744	Military victory
August 1744	Military victory
September 1744	Health of king
September 1744	Health of king
December 1744	Military victory
December 1744	Military victory
December 1744	Military victory
December 1744	Health of king
June 1745	Military victory
July 1745	Military victory
August 1745	Military victory
August 1745	Military victory
August 1745	Military victory
September 1745 (several)	Military victory
October 1745	Military victory
October 1745	Military victory
November 1745	Military victory
December 1745	Military victory
March 1746	Military victory
June 1746	Military victory
August 1746	Military victory
August 1746	Military victory
October 1746	Military victory
November 1746	Military victory
July 1747	Military victory

TABLE 4 (*cont.*)

Date	Occasion
September 1747	Military victory
February 1749	Peace
September 1751	Royal birth
September 1752	Health of the dauphin
September 1753	Royal birth
September 1754	Penitents
November 1754	Royal birth
January 1755	Penitents
December 1755	Royal birth
June 1756	Military victory
January 1757	Health of king
January 1757	Health of king
January 1757	Health of king
January 1757	Health of king
January 1757	Health of king
February 1757	Health of king
March 1757	Military victory
October 1757	Royal birth
November 1757	Royal birth
March 1758	New altar at Jesuits
September 1758	Pilgrimage of penitents
November 1758	Military victory
November 1758	Military victory
June 1759	Military victory
September 1759	New vicar-general
May 1761	Military victory
September 1762	Reception of relic
September 1762	Military victory
July 1763	Peace
November 1766	New bells at palace
April 1769	Canonization of saint
July 1769	New pope
July 1770	Reception of relics
July 1775	Coronation of Louis XVI
July 1779	Royal birth
September 1780	Military victory

at the town of Ath were truncated: the Te Deum at the cathedral was still sung as mandated, but the "feux de joie" that normally followed the church service were canceled because of the severity of the *vent d'autan*, Languedoc's celebrated seasonal wind.[26] In December two Te Deums marked the taking of Valenza and other Piedmontese strongholds.[27]

Although the ensemble of ceremonies made the public aware of the successive military campaigns waged by their king, the heart of the ceremonial, its moment of solemnity—the Te Deum—was closed off from its participation. The capitouls, parlementaires, and other notables of the city alone marched to the cathedral to attend the religious service. General processions, long the distinctive feature of urban ceremonial, marked neither a military triumph nor a declaration of peace in the latter part of the eighteenth century. The public presumably enjoyed the bonfires, illuminations, and occasional fireworks, but the triumphant ritual of thanksgiving, a moment of communion among the municipal elite, the attendant clergy, and God, took place in a closed arena.

Other celebrations of a political nature were more open to the populace, although here it is questionable whether ordinary people participated in a very meaningful way. The years between 1738 and 1780 in Toulouse were punctuated by at least ten great and prolonged festive moments, most celebrating events relating to the monarchy, its interests, and the royal family. Four—including three occasions that in fact had little to do with the city—were identified as "Fêtes de la Ville": Louis XV's recovery from illness in 1744; the peace concluded with Portugal and England in 1763; the reestablishment of the parlement in 1775; and the queen's recovery from an illness in 1779. A fifth occasion, the first entry of the duc de Richelieu into Toulouse in 1741, provoked festivities that were in scale and kind, if not in name, a Fête de la Ville as well.[28]

[26] 699:190–201.   [27] 699:203.

[28] For descriptions of the festivities mounted to celebrate various events

Let us reconstruct one of these great fetes, the Fête de la Ville staged for the recovery of Louis XV in August and September 1744. On August 28 news that the king had emerged from his prolonged illness at Metz reached Toulouse and was immediately announced to the city with the usual flourish by the Watch. Two days later the parlement gathered at the cathedral to hear a Te Deum. The tower of the parlement's palace was illuminated; bells throughout the city pealed day and night. That evening the first president hosted a dinner for his colleagues, all of whom illuminated their hôtels and lit bonfires in front of their doors. While the magistrates dined, two fountains ran with wine for the crowd that gathered around the first president's residence. On August 31 it was the archbishop's turn to honor the king's health with a dinner party for the parlementaires and their wives. The evening culminated with illuminations and bonfires. The first four days of September were marked by festivities offered by several religious orders: many convents were illuminated and the Benedictines constructed a platform jutting out over the Garonne on which a "prodigious" number of lamps was displayed. September 4 was dominated by the festivities sponsored by the merchants of the Bourse de Commerce, who earlier that day had had a Te Deum sung in the king's honor. Their building, decorated with illuminations, laurels, and Chinese lanterns, displayed on its main facade a portrait of the king crowned with laurels and surrounded by angels. The square in front of the Bourse was the scene of a *feu de joie*, accompanied by rounds of musketry. All of the merchants lit bonfires in front of their homes. On September 6 the capitouls had a Te Deum sung in the Hôtel de Ville's chapel, followed by a military salute by the Watch. From September 6 to 9 various

---

during the reign of Louis XVI, see Alain-Charles Gruber, *Les grandes fêtes et leurs décors à l'époque de Louis XVI* (Geneva, 1972).

religious orders staged celebrations, mostly illuminations, including a fireworks display sponsored by the Jesuits. All of these festivities merely prepared the city for the main event. On September 24 commenced the Fête de la Ville proper, its centerpiece a gigantic fireworks display designed by Guillaume Cammas, the city's official architect. The structure, supported by a base fifteen feet high and two hundred feet in circumference, consisted of a fifty-foot pyramid topped by several figures—principally a representation of the near-prostrate king at Metz, "in the form of a young hero ready to expire, like Alexander at Tardes," resting on a pile of laurels. Latin inscriptions covered the pyramid; "The Father of his country restored," proclaimed the main one. Lanterns joined with fleurs-de-lis, bonfires, and other devices illuminated the Hôtel de Ville and the Place Royale. More inscriptions, devices, lanterns, and a giant portrait of the king graced the Collège de Saint-Martial, whose facade fronted on the square. Surrounding the fireworks were three fountains, embellished with mythical figures, running with wine day and night. Rounds of military salutes were heard throughout the festivities, accompanied, according to Barthès, with cries of "Vive le Roy!"

The next day, September 27, the Freemasons added their festive offering to the celebrations honoring the king.[29] In the newly constructed Place d'Esplanade they elevated a forty-foot pyramid crowned by three figures, the central one a representation of Harpocrates, the "goddess presiding over their sect," posed with finger to her lips. The second was the "Goddess of Health" proffering a cup entwined with serpents, signifying the remedy given to the king. The third figure depicted the "Angel of France," crowned with flowers, trumpeting the

[29] The Freemasons' contribution to the festivities is described by Michel Taillefer in his *La franc-maçonnerie Toulousaine*, pp. 205–9; he too bases his description on Barthès's account.

news of the king's recovery. The base of this pyramidal platform took the form of a large rock harboring two grottoes, presumably signifying, like the mythical figure Harpocrates, the secret nature of the Freemasons' order. Their celebration climaxed with fireworks.

The festival of 1744 and the other Fêtes de la Ville were unprecedented in the city's history: no other municipal celebrations past or present, neither the great royal entries of the sixteenth century nor the May 17 general procession in 1762, could match them in scale, variety, and duration. But in addition to these five Fêtes de la Ville, there were yet other great festive moments during these years, moments when, for secular reasons, the city was similarly plunged into prolonged and varied celebrations. We have already noted one: the recovery from illness of President Bastard in 1739, an unexampled and indeed unique ceremonial tribute to a local official. The others marked episodes in the life of the monarch and the royal family: the birth of the dauphin in 1753; the birth of another royal son, the duc de Berry, in 1754; the king's escape from the assassination attempt in 1757; and Louis XVI's coronation in 1775.

As varied as these festive moments were, they shared several features, the most obvious being a preoccupation with the vicissitudes of the monarch's life, their essentially political nature. Others were more novel features in the realm of Old Regime ceremonial, warranting the conclusion that the period from Louis XIV's reign onward—when these sorts of fetes became common—witnessed the emergence of a new festive regime. First is their prolonged duration and massive scale, dwarfing any religious ritual in the city's calendar, even the great general processions. The Fête de la Ville for the recovery of Louis XV in 1744 took up the entire month of September; that for the reestablishment of the parlement in 1774 ran for two weeks. The celebrations in honor of the duc de Richelieu in 1741 lasted over three weeks. Other lesser political festivities were more limited in duration but still extended over several days at least, often longer. Much of January 1757, for example, was devoted to celebrating Louis XV's escape from the mortal intent of Damiens's knife. These festive moments, in short, could bring the business of the city to a virtual standstill for weeks at a time. Of course, one aspect of the city's business was precisely its ceremonial and festive offerings, which, in attracting thousands of visitors, routinely filled its inns to capacity and lined the pockets of its merchants as well.

During virtually every one of these great festive occasions, the activities were not limited to the streets. Another feature of the new style of fete is thus the existence of a parallel realm of celebration to the public exercises, one that allowed the elite to socialize in their own, protected environment. These festivities, usually dinner parties and balls, were not strictly private affairs, for the elite of the city—the magistrates of the parlement and municipal officials—normally attended ex officio; but they did rigorously exclude ordinary people.[30] And their tone was decidedly refined, or at least opulent. Those offered on the occasion of the Fête de la Ville for the peace treaty with Portugal in 1763 were typical of the sort periodically enjoyed by the *haut monde Toulousain*. On one evening First President Bastard and his wife hosted a party in their town house to which all ladies and gentlemen "of condition" were invited. It was a lavish affair, with the hôtel's interior entirely redecorated with tents, balconies, tapestries, and special illuminations. Nearly two hundred diners gathered, the women served by the men. Dancing afterward continued until seven the next morning. The following day the Hôtel de

---

[30] For a similar, nearly contemporaneous case, from Paris, of the common people being forcibly—by a guard of one hundred men—excluded from a dinner and masked ball given by the secretary of the empress Marie-Thérèse, see Gruber, *Les grandes fêtes*, p. 74.

Ville was the scene for another dinner dance for a select group of notables. Barthès remarked on "the good taste of the feast, the grace with which it was served, the quantity and delicacy of meats, the beauty of the illuminations, the splendid concert that took place during the meal, and finally the variety and quality of wines and liquors served." Again there was dancing in a ballroom entirely done over for the occasion. This time the revelers held out until dawn. The following day the same celebrants regrouped at the Cordeliers' convent for the performance of a symphony, a musical form new to the eighteenth century.[31]

If the elite of Toulouse enjoyed a range of privileged pastimes during great festive moments, the authorities made sure to provide the general populace with varied amusements of their own. And these popular diversions were another important feature of eighteenth-century secular fetes. Most evenings during a Fête de la Ville saw public dancing in one of the city's main squares—not the sort of frolicking typical of carnival or neighborhood *bals populaires* but a sponsored amusement in a public space policed and condoned by the municipal authorities. On several occasions the fete was complemented by boat races on the canal or the Garonne. During others the public was offered outdoor theatrics. For the 1775 Fête de la Ville honoring the parlement's reestablishment, for example, the capitouls constructed three stages in the Place Royale: one for an orchestra, another for a performance by marionettes and actors, a third for a high-wire and juggling act.[32] Finally, wine, flowing freely from specially constructed public fountains, almost always lubricated popular participation in the festivities. If everything else failed to make people jubilant—and attune their spirits to the official celebration of their monarch's health or fortunes—alcohol could at least render them properly lighthearted.

[31] 703:132.   [32] 705:52–55.

But these profane diversions were matched by solemn religious rituals—masses and Te Deums. Thus, for at least a moment during the great eighteenth-century fetes, some of the celebrants would turn toward God, rendering thanks for the health of their king or the peace that had been proclaimed. These were, however, moments of privileged communion reserved for the elite that gathered in the cathedral—presumably on behalf of the entire urban community. It is notable that general processions, that quintessential public devotion, for centuries the traditional urban rite, were never staged on these occasions.[33]

Their centerpiece was rather the fireworks display, the great pyrotechnical marvel that seemed to overtake eighteenth-century ceremonial throughout France.[34] This was perhaps the most distinctive feature of the new fete. To be sure, fireworks, having been imported from Italy during the Renaissance and perfected at Louis XIV's Versailles, had long been mounted in France. But their scale, pyrotechnical complexity,

[33] In emphasizing the importance and scale of the monarchical fete in the eighteenth century I do not mean to argue that these festivities were unprecedented. They clearly took place in the seventeenth century (and even earlier) in Paris, and later spread to provincial cities. In 1684, for example, the birth of the duc d'Anjou occasioned fireworks and a Te Deum in Toulouse (Rosoi, *Annales de la ville de Toulouse*, 4:567). Significant, however, is the fact that by the mid-eighteenth century, the general procession is dropped as a feature of the provincial monarchical fete. In 1729, at the birth of the dauphin, a general procession was held to complement the other festivities, such as fireworks, public dancing, and the like (ibid., Supplement, pp. 58–59). On subsequent such occasions it is absent from the accounts, Barthès's and others. But in England, celebrations of monarchy did include processions, suggesting that they are emblematic of a more inclusive political culture in which a constitutional basis of royalty is still acknowledged. See Linda Colley, "The Apotheosis of George III: Loyalty, Royalty and the British Nation, 1760–1820," *Past & Present*, no. 102 (February 1984): 94–129.

[34] And throughout Europe as well: see Barbara Widenor Maggs, "The Poetry of Eighteenth-Century Fireworks Display," *Eighteenth-Century Life* 1 (June 1975): 68–71.

and the frequency of their mountings far exceeded those staged in earlier times. One indication of this is their cost: in 1643 fireworks for the occasion of the feast of Saint-Etienne, the patron of the cathedral, cost seventy-five livres; expenditures for the pyrotechnic display to celebrate the return of the parlement in 1775 totaled nearly six thousand livres.[35]

One can only assume that all this firepower and artifice translated into an impressive display which awed the populace. But on occasion the display proved more deadly than spectacular. The mishap that turned the Parisian celebrations for the marriage of the dauphin and Marie Antoinette into a disaster, killing scores of bystanders, had a harbinger in an accident that marred an earlier Toulouse fete. In 1754 a misfiring of the display for the birth of the duc de Berry injured over a hundred people and left three or four dead.[36] For the historian Mona Ozouf these festivals, and especially their reliance on pyrotechnics to impress the populace, were less than ideal sorts of civic celebration. "Decreed from above, hierarchical, artificial, coercive, and, in the long run, murderous" is her assessment.[37] Perhaps this was the case; and certainly the Revolution saw the return to a festive tradition that invited greater participation on the part of the citizenry. But one must not dismiss the enthralling effects of a great fireworks display as mere artifice, for these were impressive technical achievements combining sophisticated pyrotechnics with architectural and sculptural splendors. Like the Montgolfiers' hot-air aviation experiments that awed crowds in Paris, Toulouse, and elsewhere in the mid-1780s (and which were frequently launched amid festive gatherings), they represented

[35] J. Lestrade, "Le feu d'artifice de Saint-Etienne," *Revue historique de Toulouse* 2 (1915–1919): 168; F. Galabert, "Feux d'artifices et collations capitulaires (1770)," *Bulletin de la Société Archéologique du Midi de la France* 40 (1909): 21–22; Archives départementales, Haute-Garonne, C 414.

[36] 702:21–22.

[37] Ozouf, *Festivals and the French Revolution,* p. 4.

another of those novel achievements so often paraded before an impressionable eighteenth-century public. Moreover, the Latin mottoes that always graced the fireworks scaffolding provided educated spectators with an edifying text to decode amid the smoke and flame, while those not versed in Latin were reminded that there was more to the ceremony than met their eyes. To be sure, royalty did not have a monopoly on fireworks, but they were emblematic of the monarch's power and grandeur, for only the king—like his counterparts throughout eighteenth-century Europe—could regularly call forth such technically impressive theatrics in all provinces of his realm. Fireworks were the ultimate "big-man" display; they were the chief medium for representing the triumph of "le roi-machine" to his people. While the king's image loomed above the city amid the sound, light, and smoke that suggested supernatural power, the populace gathered below as an undifferentiated crowd. For unlike traditional urban rituals, such as the procession (and also the royal entry), the city did not represent itself corporately on these occasions. The populace gathered to be amused and perhaps awed—to celebrate their monarch, but not to celebrate their city, or even to acknowledge ritually the corporative, hierarchical social order that was still a reality at the end of the Old Regime. Rather, the king's triumph effectively negated such self-representation—further proof of his power and "absoluteness." Two questions remain, however. How effective was this ceremonial idiom in instilling in the populace the monarchical image it attempted to convey? What was lost in these festivities that more traditional urban rituals, especially the procession, embodied?

CONCLUSION

THINKING ABOUT
THE CEREMONIAL
CITY

WHAT SHOULD we make of the ceremonial regime that Pierre Barthès has allowed us to reconstruct? How to think of it as more than one more strange feature of Old Regime culture— to be sure, not as strange as cat massacres or the rites of misrule, but perplexing to a modern sensibility nevertheless? Our informant on the public pastimes of his native city, Barthès supplies us the raw material for an analysis. But in truth he is a less than ideal informant, for his commentary on various public displays is limited: rarely does he express more than satisfaction or enthusiasm at their execution, sometimes his disappointment. He does not tell us what he or his neighbors thought about these ceremonies, what meanings they ascribed to them, whether they were crucial or merely marginal experiences in their lives. And this is why we shall have to resort to speculation, aided in part by theorizing borrowed from anthropology, in order to answer some of these questions.

One thing, however, is clear, even without Barthès's comment. In the eighteenth-century city, on the eve of the French Revolution, the weight of ceremony had not diminished since earlier times. On the contrary, it seems that the variety and sheer number of public displays increased in the last century of the Old Regime, if only because the period was heir to several centuries of ceremonial creativity. The Old Regime rarely discarded anything in the way of ritual and ceremony; indeed, it would take the Revolution to perform a major housecleaning of public life in this respect. The accretion of ceremony paralleled the accumulation of corporate and bureaucratic layers in the Old Regime: just as, for example, offices pullulated over the generations as the crown created them in successive waves of bureaucratic innovation or fiscal desperation, so too were different rites and ceremonies added to the repertoire of public life by successive cultural, religious, and political movements. The religious revival of the late Middle Ages, the Wars of Religion, the Counter-Reformation, the monarchy of Louis XIV, as well as earlier epochs in the city's past, each deposited something in the way of ceremony, so that by the later part of the eighteenth century the city's calendar of ceremonial events was more crowded than ever before.

Thus, insofar as the eighteenth-century city was "modern," it still proved hospitable to a weighty ceremonial regime. Max Weber viewed modernity as antithetical to the "enchantment" of ceremony and ritual, and the modern city as the premier locus of an unceremonial world. But this assessment, it seems, suffers from an underestimation of the durability and malleability of ceremonial forms in a modern environment.[1] And it fails to consider the importance of ceremony in legitimating a quintessential feature of the modern world: the centralized state. Yet, as we have seen, provincial Toulouse, like other French cities in the late eighteenth century, was dense in symbolic displays representing the monarchy and its interests.[2] Of

[1] Max Weber, *The City*, trans. Don Martindale and Gertrud Neuwirth (Glencoe, Ill., 1958). For an explicit critique of Weber in this sense, see Trexler, *Public Life in Renaissance Florence*, p. xxii. On the theme of the positive relationship between ritual and modernity in an early modern urban context, see also Natalie Zemon Davis, "The Sacred and the Body Social in Sixteenth-Century Lyon," *Past & Present*, no. 90 (1981): 40–70.

[2] On this theme for early modern England, see David Cressy, *Bells and Bonfires: National Memory and the Protestant Calendar in Elizabethan and*

course, the modernity of prerevolutionary France is hotly debated,[3] and a city such as Toulouse, with a weak industrial base and heavily invested in traditional institutions, was probably less modern than most. Still, it was sufficiently large, developed, and cosmopolitan to serve as a test case for the Weberian expectation that ceremony wanes as the modern city emerges. In short, Toulouse's ceremonial regime remained robust and varied, just as it did in other eighteenth-century cities. And large-scale political rites and festivities would continue to flourish in the nineteenth and twentieth centuries, especially as the modern state, in both its republican and totalitarian embodiments, gained ascendancy over public life throughout the Western world.

IF Barthès is a less than satisfactory commentator on the ceremonial regime he so attentively observed, many of his contemporaries were more forthcoming. The eighteenth century abounded with critics of festive life,[4] chief among them Rousseau. Indeed, from Rousseau to Mona Ozouf the eighteenth-century fete has been found lacking—alienated from the people, excessively preoccupied with artifice, ineffective in conveying a sense of community. Rousseau, of course, had an alternative, rather idealized sort of fete in mind when he made his criticisms—the small-scale festival among neighbors or villagers that celebrated fellowship and civic virtue. "Plant a

---

Stuart England (Berkeley, 1989), and Linda Colley, Britons: Forging the Nation 1707–1837 (New Haven and London, 1992).

[3] In a sense, the long-standing, although somewhat dépassé, debate over whether eighteenth-century France was still a feudal society is about the century's modernity. For a forceful presentation of prerevolutionary France as a modern, and modernizing, society, see Schama, Citizens.

[4] Jean Ehrard, "Les lumières et la fête," Annales historiques de la Revolution Française 87 (1975): 356–74. See also Harry Payne, "The Philosophes and Popular Ritual: Turgot, Voltaire, Rousseau," Studies in Eighteenth-Century Culture 14 (1985): 307–16.

stake crowned with flowers in the middle of a square; gather
the people together, and you will have a festival," he writes, in
a famous passage in the *Letter to Monsieur d'Alembert*. "Do
better yet: let the spectators become an entertainment to
themselves; make them actors themselves; do it so that each
sees and loves himself in the others so that all will be better
united."[5]

But in reality, as opposed to the utopian musings of Rousseau and his followers, the eighteenth-century fete should be
contrasted, not with the Maypole celebration or some other
such rustic rites, but with the religious rituals that had long
marked public life in the Old Regime city, especially the procession. Early modern historians usually emphasize the emerging split between local and popular festive life, on the one
hand, and its rival, those political and religious ceremonies
representing national concerns and elite values, on the other.[6]
As central as this was to the transformation of traditional culture, it should not obscure a similar, perhaps later, development, pitting secular festivities against religious ritual, much
of it based in Counter-Reformation Catholicism.[7] I have argued for the ubiquity of the procession as a form of religious
ritual, even in the eighteenth century when there are indica-
tions that its mobilizing potential began to wane. Whether its
strength as an urban ritual declined or not, it clearly had a
rival in the politically oriented festivals that dominated the

[5] *Politics and the Arts: Letter to M. D'Alembert on the Theatre*, trans. Allan
Bloom (Ithaca, 1960), p. 126.

[6] For a summary, see Chartier et al., *La ville classique*, pp. 180–98; and for
England, Peter Borsay, "'All the town's a stage': Urban Ritual and Cere-
mony 1660–1800," in *The Transformation of English Provincial Towns*, ed.
Peter Clark (London, 1984), pp. 228–58.

[7] For an analysis that appreciates this particular conflict, see Annie Lama-
don, "Les fêtes civiques dans le Département du Puy-de-Dôme sous la
Révolution," in *La Révolution dans Le Puy-de-Dôme*, ed. A. Soboul, Com-
mission d'histoire économique et sociale de la Révolution Française (Paris,
1972), pp. 265–83. I owe this reference to Ted Margadant.

city in the last century of the Old Regime. An understanding of the ceremonial city would thus seem to entail a comparison between these two sorts of public ceremonies. Might we refer to them as two contrasting ceremonial idioms?[8] Religious processions and political festivities competed for the populace's attention in the eighteenth-century city. What did these very different idioms mean for the articulation of Toulouse's public life?

The first and most obvious difference is the pretext for their staging. Processions were mounted for myriad occasions, from funerals and natural disasters to the great religious feasts that regularly marked the church calendar. They were collective appeals or acts of thanksgiving to God. Though processions were essentially forms of public devotion, their ritual meanings were not confined to the spiritual realm. For they were also communal ceremonies, assembling the various members of the municipal order in what was meant to be a single, coordinated display. And when the urban community processed each year on May 17 to commemorate the "deliverance" of their city in 1562, the ceremony was indeed as much in celebration of the triumph of Toulouse as of the True Faith. By contrast, the eighteenth-century fete vaunted the monarchy and the royal family or celebrated France's military victories. Only rarely did the celebratory moment have some relationship to the city or its institutions. These repeated moments of great festivity exposed to the general populace the triumphs and travails of their monarch, framing the image of his person with classical allusions and pyrotechnical marvels. We can only assume that the size and complexity of these displays dazzled onlookers, that the people appreciated, or at least en-

---

[8] For a model analysis of how two different ritual "languages"—in this case Catholicism and Calvinism—organized, both temporally and spatially, urban life, see Davis, "The Sacred and the Body Social in Sixteenth-Century Lyon."

joyed, the officially sanctioned amusements that always accompanied them. Although historians have argued persuasively for a decline in the monarch's prestige in the decades before the Revolution, one must not discount the possibility that such extravagance also translated into an appreciation for the monarchy itself, resulting in a heightened awe, even respect, for the king and his powers. Church ritual had long held a monopoly over symbolic representations on the public stage. In the eighteenth century expressions of royalty and royal power—essentially secular ceremonies, complemented, to be sure, with devotional exercises—dominated the urban scene as never before, eclipsing in size and novelty virtually all religious displays.

These two types of ceremony differed as well in the manner of their organization in terms of space and time. The procession was, of course, ambulatory: it traversed the cityscape and crossed the city's major axes. It marked the city with its devotional and communal messages. If it did not enter every neighborhood, the procession at least recognized its major monuments—the Saint-Sernin basilica, the cathedral, the Hôtel de Ville, the parlementary palace—and thus acknowledged with its peripatetic presence the particular city that was Toulouse. The Fête de la Ville and the other major secular festivities had a rather different spatial orientation. They were stationary, fixed in a central square, usually the Place Royale. And it is important to note that this large space in front of the Hôtel de Ville, located at the city's center, had only been cleared out and renovated in the mid-eighteenth century. It was an anonymous space by its very configuration and location, detached from the traditional, still largely medieval cityscape, virtually identical to other ceremonial squares throughout urban France. The eighteenth-century fete merely took place *in* the city, perhaps subsuming it with its festive abundance, but not inhabiting it as the general procession did.

Staged in the aptly named Place Royale, these festivities reproduced in the provincial capital a facsimile of that "vital center"
which ruled France from Versailles.[9]

A similar difference can be observed in the two ceremonials'
temporal orientation. Although many religious celebrations
were extraordinary occasions provoked by a special event—the
election of a new pope, the canonization of a saint, and the
like—most belonged to the calendar of fixed Catholic feast
and holy days. The four general processions were staged at the
same time each year; religious orders, parish churches, hospitals, craft and lay confraternities, and other corporations also
regularly took to the streets to fete their patron saints. The
four penitential companies undertook their pilgrimages at regular intervals as well. In short, the rhythm of processions and
other public devotions was for the most part predictable,
marking the city's ceremonial calendar in a way that temporally organized public life. Moreover, many of these processions commemorated events in Toulouse's history, especially
the period of the religious wars, and thus were rooted in the
city's past. The secular fete, on the other hand, escaped both
the constraints of the past and those of the calendar. It celebrated the triumphant present, never the past, demonstrating,

---

[9] "Such centers, which have 'nothing to do with geometry and little with
geography,' are essentially concentrated loci of serious acts; they consist in
the point or points in a society where its leading ideas come together with
its leading institutions to create an arena in which the events that most
vitally affect its members' lives take place. It is involvement, even opposi-
tional involvement, with such arenas and with the momentous events that
occur in them that confers charisma. It is a sign, not of popular appeal or
inventive craziness, but of being near the heart of things." Geertz, "Centers,
Kings, and Charisma: Reflections on the Symbolics of Power," in *Local
Knowledge* (New York, 1983), pp. 122–23. Two recent studies that deal with
this issue are Avner Ben-Amos, "The Sacred Center of Power: Paris and the
Republican State Funerals," *Journal of Interdisciplinary History* 22, no. 1
(1991): 27–48; and James Von Geldern, *Bolshevik Festivals, 1917–1920* (Berkeley, Los Angeles, and London, 1993), chap. 6.

as Peter Borsay has observed, that for royalty "the present proved more interesting than the past."[10] The secular fete was imposed upon the city according to the vicissitudes of royal life at Versailles, the martial fortunes of the king's armies, and other interests of state. And not only Toulouse: cities and towns throughout the realm simultaneously feted the monarchy on these occasions, which were thereby moments of national celebration. The city's relationship to these fetes was thus reactive, its ceremonial life increasingly governed by unpredictable and distant events. If religious rituals served to organize the calendar of public life, the secular fetes often interrupted it.

One can thus speak of the secular fete in terms of its alienation from the traditional strictures of ceremonial life. A similar sort of alienation was reflected in its social organization. The procession was a public devotion that enlisted the active participation of the faithful; and the general procession raised its level of participation to a communal level. To be sure, the procession was hierarchical and corporative in organization; even the general procession excluded many sorts of people—those, for example, who had no place in the urban order of corps and institutions. But many others relegated to the sidelines could at least vicariously identify with the ceremony by virtue of the participation of groups and institutions that represented them. The procession, in short, fostered active participation on the part of a range of people, from royal magistrates to the city poor. The secular fete, by contrast, transformed these same people into spectators. There was plenty to do during a Fête de la Ville—games and outdoor theatrics to enjoy, fireworks to gawk at, wine to drink—but none of these amusements called for the public to be anything beyond a crowd of consumers. The only true actors on the festive scene

[10] Borsay, "'All the town's a stage,'" p. 232.

during these citywide celebratory moments were members of the officialdom, both royal and municipal, who at least were granted the privilege of hearing the Te Deum in the cathedral. If the general procession attempted to encompass the municipal community in a ritual display, the secular fete forsook such an attempt, yielding to two parallel tendencies in eighteenth-century cultural life—the increasing emphasis on entertainment, and the creation of separate realms for polite, upper-class sociability.

This point needs to be stressed, for one current view has it that the eighteenth century did not exhibit the kind of social divide between the elite and popular realms that historians like Peter Burke and others have asserted as a fundamental feature of contemporary cultural life.[11] In particular, Robert Isherwood and Simon Schama have argued that in the latter part of the century there emerged entertainments and spectacles that created venues for mixed sociability.[12] In the new Parisian entertainments Isherwood reconstructs—marketplace performances, street fairs, Waux-Halls, and the carnivalesque milieu of the Palais-Royal—he observes a "convergence of popular and elite culture." Schama claims that festive gatherings such as those attending the Montgolfiers' balloon launchings demonstrate that popular culture transcended the hierarchical strictures that had characterized Old Regime ritual, thus bolstering his general argument that prerevolutionary France had already gone some distance in opening up and reforming public and political life.

[11] Burke, *Popular Culture*, pp. 270–80; Robert Muchembled, *Culture populaire et culture des élites dans la France moderne, XVe–XVIIIe siècles: essai* (Paris, 1978); David Garrioch, *Neighborhood and Community in Paris, 1740–1790* (Cambridge, 1986), chap. 5; Thomas Brennan, *Public Drinking and Popular Culture in Eighteenth-Century Paris* (Princeton, 1988); Schneider, *Public Life in Toulouse*.

[12] Isherwood, *Farce and Fantasy: Popular Entertainment in Eighteenth-Century Paris* (New York, 1986); Schama, *Citizens*, pp. 123–44.

What does the evidence from eighteenth-century Toulouse demonstrate regarding the "fashionable popular/elite distinction"?[13] On one level Barthès's diary furnishes ample proof that this distinction was in fact quite relevant to cultural life. We have noted, for example, that virtually every occasion of a Fête de la Ville or other secular festival was complemented with private dinner parties, symphony concerts, and costume balls reserved for the exclusive enjoyment of the municipal elite and officialdom. The very tone of these entertainments spoke in terms of an elite with cultivated tastes, or at least pretensions. And while these ladies and gentlemen making up *le monde toulousain* amused themselves behind closed doors, the city provided suitable entertainments—free-flowing wine, fireworks, acrobatic acts, and other street performances—for the rest of the populace. If the popular-elite distinction was so outmoded, as Isherwood and Schama have claimed, why was it asserted so self-consciously at moments such as these?

On another level, however, it cannot be denied that many eighteenth-century entertainments demonstrated a novel ability to captivate a wide public, upper and lower classes alike. There were indeed no class or corporate distinctions in the crowds that gathered on the occasion of a Fête de la Ville, no prescribed behavior mandated by the celebration, no barriers excluding certain groups of people from the festivities. Even the novel, somewhat occult Freemasons could gain a place in the fete. Moreover, the very venue of these festivities had changed. Here I want to stress something I have mentioned in passing several times. As a result of the urbanist movement, public space in Toulouse (as in other French cities) was significantly altered and expanded in the last decades before the Revolution.[14] These changes were far-ranging, and Barthès

[13] Isherwood, *Farce and Fantasy,* p. 38.
[14] On the new public spaces and the eighteenth-century urbanist movement, see Pierre Lavedan, *Histoire de l'urbanisme,* vol. 2, *Renaissance et temps*

proves a keen, sometimes critical observer of most of them. But the most significant was the clearing out and opening up of large public squares in several parts of the city, most prominently the Place Royale in front of the Hôtel de Ville, an area that still serves as Toulouse's central plaza. While the urbanists were concerned with public salubrity, economic development, and the rational use of space, these areas also provided new and vastly expanded arenas for urban ceremony. All of the main celebrations and pyrotechnic displays associated with the Fêtes de la Ville were staged in the Place Royale (as were the May 17th fireworks in 1762). Indeed, these gigantic festivities would have been inconceivable without the new public space that now accommodated them.

An expanded arena for urban sociability was as significant as the festivities that occasionally took place there. For it relates to the subject of an eighteenth-century "public," a concept that a number of historians have treated mostly in the context of emerging sociable and discursive forms that challenged the hierarchial values and closed venues of the Old Regime.[15] But this somewhat abstract notion of the public also

---

modernes (Paris, 1953); Chartier et al., *La ville classique*, pp. 439–82; Perrot, *Genèse d'une ville moderne*; Henri Michel, "Urbanisme et société à Montpellier sous l'Ancien Régime," *Annales du Midi* 86 (1974): 21–43; Line Teisseyre Sallmann, "Urbanisme et société: l'exemple de Nîmes aux XVIIe et XVIIIe siècles," *Annales: ESC* 35 (1980): 965–86; Schneider, *Public Life in Toulouse*, pp. 344–52.

[15] Jurgen Habermas, *L'espace publique: archéologie de la publicité comme dimension constitutive de la société bourgeoise* (Paris, 1986); Mona Ozouf, "L'opinion publique," in Baker, *The Political Culture of the Old Regime*, pp. 419–34; Keith M. Baker, "Politics and Public Opinion under the Old Regime: Some Reflections," in *Press and Politics in Pre-Revolutionary France*, ed. Jack R. Censer and Jeremy D. Popkin (Berkeley and Los Angeles, 1987), pp. 204–46, and idem, "Defining the Public Sphere in Eighteenth-Century France: Variations on a Theme by Habermas," in *Habermas and the Public Sphere*, ed. Craig Calhoun (Cambridge, Mass., 1972), pp. 181–211. Two insightful reviews of literature on this issue are Anthony J. La Vopa, "Con-

had a physical corollary in new terrains for public interaction.[16] For example, Thomas Crow's study of the new art salons that emerged in the second half of the century demonstrates an interest not only in novel aesthetic enterprises but also in venues that could invite a genuine public "to rehearse before works of art the kinds of pleasure and discrimination that once had been the exclusive prerogative of the patron and his intimates."[17] Isherwood's fairs and theaters also provided a context for the gathering of a mixed public of curious pleasure-seekers. These were real spaces that drew eighteenth-century Parisians into new places, offering the possibility of novel patterns of public interaction. And so too were the outdoor public spaces created in Toulouse and other French cities that opened up the cityscape for congregating crowds, both informal and festive. Invited to these spaces by repeated secular festivities, the crowd was thus provided with a venue that, unlike the highly structured processional context, allowed for the freest sort of public sociability.

---

ceiving a Public: Ideas and Society in Eighteenth-Century Europe," *Journal of Modern History* 64 (March 1992): 79–116; and Dena Goodman, "Public Sphere and Private Life: Toward a Synthesis of Current Historiographical Approaches to the Old Regime," *History and Theory* 31 (1992): 1–20.

[16] I am aware that, as formulated by Habermas, the dialectical process of the emergence of an eighteenth-century public entailed a transformation of private, "intersubjective" activities—from the reading of novels to conversation—into a discursive ideal that stood in opposition to the supposedly closed, secret realm of courtly or monarchical culture. My use of the concept of the public has thus little in common with the precise terms of this formulation; neither does it relate to the importance of criticism as a feature of public opinion, nor is it limited to a class—quite the contrary.

[17] Thomas E. Crow, *Painters and Public Life in Eighteenth-Century Paris* (New Haven and London, 1985), p. 3. An annual art exhibit, which also invited a rather broad public, was initiated in Toulouse in 1751. Barthès comments that "there men and women, people of every age and condition, can go see the most beautiful works of art that have been collected from many different sources" (700:36).

But the crowd was not left to its own devices, for, especially in the eighteenth century, such congregating could prove contentious and violent as well. Thus, as Colin Lucas has argued, public space was problematic ground in the Old Regime.[18] It was subject to monarchical control, if only because it offered the populace an arena for protest and potentially free expression; indeed, the crown strove mightily to preempt popular mobilization, not only in the interest of public order, but as ultimate proof of its absolute power. The crowd, however, was not only controlled, it was also convoked, for the crown's political authority ultimately required the people's participation as witness to its ceremonial representations. Thus, in the newly constructed plazas was reproduced in countless French cities that "vital center"—far from its geographical locus of Versailles—that Geertz has judged an essential feature of political culture. But this center was not only the privileged arena for the "charismatic" representation of the monarch; it was also the stage for celebratory gatherings that were relatively free of traditional constraints on public sociability. It was in this public space that eighteenth-century ceremonial life, monarchical authority, and popular mobilization converged.

The crowd was convoked for many sorts of occasions, not only for these festive displays celebrating the monarch and his fortunes. And if nothing else, Barthès's diary reminds us of the constant congregating that was an essential feature of public life in the Old Regime. The general public was convened to witness displays of criminal justice, sanctioning by its very presence the legal authority that had its way with the bodies of those deemed worthy of punishment. The faithful were repeatedly convened to demonstrate their faith in processions

---

[18] Colin Lucas, "The Crowd and Politics between *Ancien Régime* and Revolution in France," *Journal of Modern History* 3 (1988): 421–57.

that also testified to their membership in a variety of communities—that of their church, their confraternity or corporation, and their city. And the king's subjects were convened to celebrate his health and good fortune in festivities that licensed an almost carnivalesque gathering in the shadow of his image.

Each occasion, however, implied a different protocol governing the people's participation; each ceremony gave rise to a different celebratory idiom. This is most obvious in the comparison between processions and political festivities. The procession, I have argued, entailed a high degree of coordination, often among vastly different groups and institutions. Sometimes the coordination failed, creating a scene of public disruption and contention during what was to have been a sacred ritual. It is impossible to know whether people and officials appreciated the risk inherent in processions, large and small; but it seems reasonable to assume that this risk endowed the collective ritual with a psychological payoff that, adding to its religious and social significance, ensured its centrality in the Old Regime ceremonial. The processional dynamic, in short, was defined by a creative tension that was inherent in the rite's performative dimension. Secular festivities, on the other hand, did not draw upon people's coordinated participation, did not oblige them to join ranks in a ritual demonstration of the urban community's integrity and unity. To be sure, such activities as fireworks, games, public dancing, and the like required planning, coordination, and a collective will on the part of the participants to maintain order and decorum. And fireworks in particular could be dangerous; one should not underestimate the degree of risk that such technically challenging spectacles entailed. But this was not the same sort of social risk that hung over a mass procession. The obvious corollary to this suggestion—difficult to prove but logically consistent—is that the secular fete, risk-free in terms of a socially embarrassing breakdown, thereby lacked the capacity either to project ceremonially an image of the urban community or to involve the populace in a ritualistic event.

All of this is to view the secular fete as lacking in the emotive power presumably conveyed by more traditional celebrations—a decidedly Rousseauist assessment. But clearly the new festivities offered a degree of freedom and openness that traditional religious rituals in fact strove to preempt. While I would insist, *pace* Isherwood and Schama, that this did not amount to a transcendence of the split between popular and elite cultures, it did conform to other eighteenth-century trends tending toward a relaxation of formal constraints in various domains. Two are especially germane because they relate to the conceptual ordering of public space. One was the ideology—and intermittently the royal policy—of relaxing constraints on the grain trade. While this may seem somewhat removed from the subject of public festivals, the champions of a free market were in fact concerned not only with economic liberty but with modifying the policing apparatus that controlled public space. This was indeed the perception of such opponents of liberalization as the abbé Galiani, who explicitly linked the disaster attending the Parisian celebration for the marriage of Marie Antoinette and the dauphin—a disaster he blamed on criminally lax policing—with the deregulation policies of the *économistes*.[19] For liberalizing the grain trade meant relaxing the governing constraints on public space. It is important to note as well that many of the urbanists, those proponents of the opening up and clearing out of the cityscape, were inspired in part by physiocratic, free-trade principles.[20] The other analogous trend may seem even more farfetched,

[19] Steven L. Kaplan, *La Bagarre: Galiani's "Lost" Parody* (The Hague, 1979).
[20] Schneider, *Public Life in Toulouse*, pp. 344–52.

but it too relates to changing conceptions of space. This was a shift in French gardening practices. Until the mid-eighteenth century, the prevailing fashion followed the "French" mode—formal, stylized, Cartesian. Then, as in many other domains, the English fashion became the rage: gardens were cultivated to assume a "natural" look, no longer encumbered with severe geometric constraints but rather designed to replicate an authentic pastoral setting. While the English-style garden was the result of just as much cultivation as the French, it was intended to project the image of nature freely left to its own sublime design. In both cases—economic liberalization and a shift to a more "natural" style of gardening—the underlying ethos was similar: a rejection of constraints that inhibited vital, creative forces. While the architects of secular festivities did not articulate such guiding principles, the results in terms of public sociability were largely the same.

In this sense, secular festivities should be seen as indicative of a widespread eighteenth-century trend away from the formality and social constraints that traditionally governed Old Regime culture. The procession embodied these traditional patterns. On the one hand it was rigorously structured both hierarchically and corporatively, when these sorts of social divisions were seen by many as having become archaic in a changing, dynamic society; on the other it was a communal rite, joining citizens both high and low in common purpose, when such social mixing in the streets struck many as distasteful, unwarranted, and unbecoming of their status. By contrast, secular festivities created a sort of free zone in the arena of public life. To repeat Maurice Bloch's formulation: Just as ordinary language enlarges the range of expressive possibilities that formal language stifles with its preordained strictures, so the secular fete enlarged the repertoire of public interaction and behavior, if only because it no longer attempted to orchestrate people's participation during these festive moments.

In this sense, the secular fete was more in keeping with the dynamics of the modern city.

The balance sheet on eighteenth-century ceremonial life was thus mixed. Perhaps not in eclipse but increasingly challenged for supremacy was a devotional regime that had deep roots in the city's culture, that often marked the cityscape with its perambulating processions, that frequently mobilized much of the urban community, that forced decorum upon its otherwise fractious members, and that created moments of heightened tension for all concerned. Secular festivities projected other qualities: spectacle, technical sophistication, entertainment, and repeated lessons in the political culture of Bourbon royalty. But how effective were they in this last sense—how well did they perform the ceremonial function of drawing the populace into identifying with their monarch? The argument I have presented here is that, whatever these festivities offered of the new and liberating, they could not match traditional religious rituals in fostering the kind of meaningful participation that might have evoked popular commitment to their ideological ends, and this for two reasons. First, they were alien to the city, imposed from without, and thus failed to breach the distance between the monarchy and the people that had been a feature of French political culture since the seventeenth century. And second, however appealing these festivities undoubtedly were as spectacle and entertainment, it cannot be said that they exerted much ritualistic force over the populace. Lacking in that performative dimension evident in the procession, they were festive gatherings whose wide appeal should not be underestimated, but not ritualistic events that held the potential to transform and galvanize the populace.

These conclusions, I hasten to add, must remain speculative. But in a sense, they find confirmation in the ceremonial history of the Revolution. For the Revolution, though certainly creative in terms of public festivities, actually drew upon traditional Old Regime ceremonies for its supposedly novel displays. In short, what we see emerging in revolutionary festivals combines the two ceremonial forms most prominent in Barthès's diary. The great revolutionary festivals, from the Feast of the Federation to the Festival of the Supreme Being, were large-scale spectacles combining art and artifice, sometimes even fireworks. Their centerpieces were stationary displays intended to instruct the populace through word and image and to impress them with their splendor and ingenuity. But these spectacles did not merely overawe a populace that gathered crowdlike before them. For virtually every revolutionary festival also included parades of citizens organized processionally as an integral part of the event itself.[21] The fetes had a theatrical element; those designed by David, as Frederick Brown writes, were "*tableaux vivants* marshalling all citizens into Jacobinism's social cosmos."[22] The people, or rather delegations representing elements of the populace, were convened to these fetes as performers, not merely observers, and

---

[21] On the processional roots of revolutionary festivals, see Ozouf, *Festivals and the French Revolution*, pp. 53, 59, 79–80. The importance of processions in these festivals was apparent to foreign sympathetic observers. An Englishman, Charles Pigott, noted in his *Political Dictionary: Explaining the Meaning of Words* (London, 1795) that "The FRENCH REPUBLIC displays all the sublimity of sentiment, all the richness of imagination, and ardour of patriotism, in those civic festivals which the Convention decrees, in honour of any splendid victory, or important advantage, which the arms of Liberty achieve over the forces of Treachery and Despotism. Magnificent processions, no longer sullied by the ignoble badges of superstition and fanaticism, but embellished with an insignia of peace, freedom, and equality, animating citizens with an invincible hatred of tyrants, and a sacred love for the divine cause in which they are engaged . . ." Quoted in Colley, "The Apotheosis of George III," p. 109.

[22] Frederick Brown, *Theater and Revolution: The Culture of the French Stage* (New York, 1989), p. 75; see also Carol Blum, *Rousseau and the Republic of Virtue: The Language of Politics in the French Revolution* (Ithaca and London, 1986), p. 250.

their role was defined by processional rites that clearly borrowed from traditional public devotions. If nothing else, this conflation of two ceremonial idioms during the Revolution suggests an implicit critique of Old Regime festivities where the performative, participatory, and ritualistic elements had been missing. The fact that the subsequent history of festive life in the West has exhibited great difficulty in maintaining both popular participation and ritual as elements of public life suggests that the problem lies in the very nature of modern culture.

In any case, it is clear from Barthès's diary that the last decades of the Old Regime saw no waning in the degree to which festivity and ritual dominated public life. Quite the contrary: one might speak of a sort of ceremonial overload, a festive and ceremonial regime marked by contradictions and tensions that did not break down until the massive breakdown of the Old Regime itself that was the French Revolution. But by then, Pierre Barthès was nearly a decade dead, in all likelihood spinning in his grave, although perhaps consoled, even gleefully so, with the realization that his ceaseless pronouncements of a coming disaster had been prophetic. It certainly would have been in character.

INDEX

absolutism, 104, 173
acampa, 64
Albigensian Crusade, 64
Alexander the Great, 167
Ambrose, Saint, 121
amende honorable, 78, 79, 96
Amsterdam, 85, 89
animal distemper epidemic, 56–57, 129
Anjou, duc d', 171n
"Annales manuscrits de la Ville de Toulouse," 30
Annonces, affiches et avis divers, 32–33, 37
anti-structure, 9. See also *communitas*
archbishop of Toulouse, 113, 127, 153, 155, 156, 160, 163, 166
art salons, 186
Ascension Day, 130
Ath, 165
Augustine, Saint, 121
Augustines, 156
Austin, J. L., 12; and theory of performative utterance, 12
Averlence, Jeanne, 17, 19

bakers, 67, 79
balloon launchings. See Montgolfiers
bals populaires. See public dancing
Baour, Jean-Florent (*Almanac historique de Toulouse*), 72
baptismal ceremony, 131–32
Barthès, Guillaume, 19
Barthès, Jean-Pierre, 19–20

Barthès, Pierre, 3, 10, 14, 15, 151, 175, 193; as Christian humanist, 39–40; his attitudes toward criminals, 86–87, 103, 107; conservatism of, 38; intellectual makeup of, 36–37; as Latinist, 49; misogyny of, 47; as municipal patriot, 32, 34; personal history and temperament of, 19–28; reactions of to religious and political conflicts, 58–62; his views on executions, 27–28, 86, 90–95, 99, 101–4, 107, 109; his views of poor, 45–46; his views of urban society, 47–50. See also "Les heures perdues"
Basoche, 67–68
Bastard (first president of parlement), 152–53, 168, 169
beatification ceremonies. See saints
Becker, Carl, 28
beheadings, 92, 97
Bell, David A., 68n
Benedictines, 130, 166
Berry, duc de, 168, 172
Bertrandi, Nicolas (*Les gestes de tholosans*), 30
Bien, David D., 3, 22, 122, 143n; *The Calas Affair*, 3
big-man displays. See big-men
big-men, 151–53, 158, 173
Black Penitents, Company of, 117, 145, 154
Black Virgin, statue of, 111–12, 127–29, 132
Bloch, Maurice, 141, 190

Robert A. Schneider is Associate Professor of History
at The Catholic University of America.
He is the author of
Public Life in Toulouse, 1463–1789.